FROM BRAY TO ETERNITY

A Memoir of a Life Shared

Annette & Andy Halpin

ORIGINAL WRITING

© 2012 ANNETTE AND ANDY HALPIN

ISBN: 978-1-908817-72-3

A CIP catalogue for this book is available from the National Library.

Published by ORIGINAL WRITING LTD., Dublin, 2012.

Printed in Great Britain by MPG BOOKS GROUP, Bodmin and Kings Lynn

Royalties from this Memoir will be donated to the Annette Halpin Memorial Music Bursary Awards for Young Musicians which is administered by South Dublin County Council.

ACKNOWLEDGEMENTS

I would like to acknowledge all the help and encouragement I've received from Orla Scannell and Blaithin Keegan of the arts department of *South Dublin County Council* in bringing this book to where it is at. Without their willingness to row in behind me and back the venture in organising the launch it would not have been possible for me to have got it done. Their commitment to keeping the Bursary Award in Annette's name going for the past two years is commendable, and their commitment to this project was and is much appreciated as was their willingness to help in organising the memorial concert of Annette's music in 2010 which was the start of the Bursary to which royalties from the sale of this book will be donated.

I also wish to thank Dave Kennedy of *The Tallaght Echo* who in the middle of a very busy period agreed to write the Foreword for me. To Fr. Derek Farrell I want to say thanks for allowing me to republish the article he wrote in the *Traveller* magazine after Annette's passing and for all his help when we staged the memorial show in 2010.To Garrett and Steven in *Original Writing* a big thank you for all your help, a special thanks to Steven for the wonderful cover design he came up with for the book.

To Annette's mother Mary, who is thankfully still with us as this is being written I want to send my love, and thank her and Bill for the gift of Annette. To Annette's sisters, Marie, Claire, Caroline and Louise and her brother Liam and all our neighbours and friends, particularly friends of Annette I wish to acknowledge all their support and good wishes over the last three years, it was very comforting and therapeutic for me to know how well thought of and loved Annette was.

I also want to acknowledge all the love and support I've received from our children, David, Gina, and Robert since Annette passed away, it has not been an easy time for them losing their mother at a stage in their lives when her support in helping them guide our grandchildren would have been invaluable, but they and their spouses Ciara and Dave have always been there for me to help and encourage me along, and with the great pleasure and joy I get from our grandchildren , Senan, Ella May, Mina and Aara, life has not been as barren as it might have been. For us all as a family, trying to live without the huge presence for good that Annette was in our lives has I believe brought us closer together.

Finally, and most of all I want to thank Annette for being in Bray on that sunny August bank holiday Sunday in 1965 when I was persuaded to forego the enjoyment of a football match, which led to a love match, and for allowing me the privilege of accompanying her on the earthly part of her journey for 44 years. It was a magical and unforgettable journey filled with love, and for still being there when I need her, as she was while we wrote this memoir.

"All is Well"

Andy Halpin.
March, 2012

Foreword

The untimely death of Annette Halpin back in 2009 brought great shock and sadness to those who knew her.

I had known Annette for many years. Not as a close friend but one who witnessed what she had achieved.

Annette will be ranked among the many unsung heroes of Tallaght. Her zest for life and the joy she brought to those around her will be remembered by many.

Tallaght is a unique place and for some reason many who came to live and settle here made huge contributions to the quality of life of their neighbours and community, Annette was one of those.

She had a passion and a desire to improve life in this community and yet she never saw herself in that way. To me she was quiet and often appeared shy and always dignified but those qualities were her gift to those around her.

In 1991 Annette joined a unique group in Tallaght. She was nominated and won Tallaght Person of the Year. This was the highest accolade anyone could achieve in our community and she won that award like so many others who have won it for her contribution to our society.

Her death brought great sadness to her family but the fullness of her life, the joy she brought to those around her will always be remembered with great fondness. She goes down in the social history of our town as one of our heroes.

David Kennedy
Managing Director
The Echo Newspaper
Dublin

Notes on the writing of "From Bray To Eternity"

From Bray To Eternity is the story of two people who over the course of 44 years became one. I had no idea that meeting a beautiful young girl in Bray in 1965 would lead me on the journey it has done, but I am so very grateful for the trip.

When Annette passed away in 2009 I was numbed by the shock and it took me several months to fully realize what had happened, that my life had changed forever and from here on I was on my own, on my own after 44 years of depending on Annette for almost everything in my daily life, a faithful confidant, companionship, encouragement, support in anything I did, sympathy, a shoulder to cry on from time to time, forgiveness, and most of all love, Annette gave me all of these things and much more, unconditionally and without complaint.

When the enormity of the change in my life began to hit home I tried in every way I knew how to bring Annette back into my life again and keep her there. One of the ways I tried to do this was by writing. I tried to remember and write down on paper how our life together began. In my mind I went back to Bray in 1965 and without ever thinking at the time that I would write a book I began to put down as accurately as I could remember, the events of our meeting. After a while I found I was remembering things that were buried deep in my mind and it was at this time that I, one day in Bohernabreena Cemetery told Annette what I was trying to do and asked for her help in doing so, immediately I got what I have described in the book as a "thought intrusion." I "heard" Annette's voice in my mind saying, "I'll be your ghost writer" it was said in a jocular way and I laughed at the idea of it.

I continued writing and it soon became obvious to me that Annette meant what she had said, as I was getting prompts from her all the time and I was amazed at what I was remembering and writing. I know this all sounds like crazy stuff, but I know it happened and I really don't care what anyone else thinks. We, (by this time I was sure Annette was helping me so I began to think of the writing as a joint venture) ploughed on with the writing of what by now I was beginning to think could be a book, and when it was finished and I read over it I was truly amazed that I had written what was on the pages, because even as I read it there were parts that I did not recollect writing, I found myself reading them as if for the first time.

I sent the draft manuscript to four or five publishers over a period of time, from two I got the manuscript back unread with notes stating that one was not interested and the other only published commissioned memoirs, from another two I got nice letters complimenting me on how well written they thought the book was and how moving they found the parts which described Annette's illness and passing and some other nice comments, but despite all their compliments they were not in a position to publish it. I let it rest for a while and then before Christmas 2011 I heard an item on Pat Kenny's radio show about self publishing and I thought it might be worthwhile to find out more about it. I approached the company mentioned on the radio show (Original Writing) and after getting further details I got the idea to self publish and donate the proceeds, if any, to keeping the Bursary fund in Annette's name going. I approached Orla Scannell, arts officer with South Dublin County Council and she was very supportive about the idea, and the rest as they say is history.

Basically this Memoir recounts our life from the moment we met at the foot of Bray Head until Annette's passing from this life in April 2009. In it I have endeavoured to present the reader with an honest and entertaining account of the many high points, and indeed the low points that we as a couple encountered and surmounted over the course of the 44 years we were together, I have written about the beginnings of our relationship and the early years of our marriage, our extensive travels which included being fired upon and evicted from our hotel at the beginning of the intifada in The Holy Land, a season as mature couriers in

France, Annette's term as Tallaght Person Of The Year in 1991, the near disintegration of our marriage and how we went about saving it and the part our time in Dingle played in saving our marriage.

I have also written about the extraordinary events that occurred before and after Annette's illness and her heroic battle with the cancer that ultimately caused her to pass from this world. The strange and inexplicable occurrences which occurred before and after Annette's passing and which indeed are still from time to time happening, convinced me, who was an unapologetic sceptic and cynic before November 2008 when they began, that life in some shape or form goes on after we depart this plain of existence, which is a great comfort as I know I will be reunited with Annette when I take my leave of this world.

In writing this book I have tried to remember that no matter how many copies of it are sold it will only ever be read by one person at a time, so I have tried to write it in an as natural and conversational tone as possible, as if I was telling our story to that one person, which at this moment is you, so enjoy the read.

Andy Halpin,
March 2012

Contents

PROLOGUE   I

CHAPTER ONE   3

CHAPTER TWO   10

CHAPTER THREE   15

CHAPTER FOUR   19

CHAPTER FIVE   22

CHAPTER SIX   26

CHAPTER SEVEN   31

CHAPTER EIGHT   35

CHAPTER NINE   41

CHAPTER TEN   47

CHAPTER ELEVEN   58

CHAPTER TWELVE   63

CHAPTER THIRTEEN   73

CHAPTER FOURTEEN   80

CHAPTER FIFTEEN   84

CHAPTER SIXTEEN   87

CHAPTER SEVENTEEN   94

CHAPTER EIGHTEEN   98

CHAPTER NINETEEN   108

CHAPTER TWENTY   113

CHAPTER TWENTY ONE   124

CHAPTER TWENTY TWO   128

CHAPTER TWENTY THREE   131

CHAPTER TWENTY FOUR   135

CHAPTER TWENTY FIVE   145

CHAPTER TWENTY SIX   152

CHAPTER TWENTY SEVEN   161

CHAPTER TWENTY EIGHT   168

CHAPTER TWENTY NINE   177

CHAPTER THIRTY   182

CHAPTER THIRTY ONE   190

CHAPTER THIRTY TWO   197

EPILOGUE   201

FROM BRAY TO ETERNITY

PROLOGUE

The loneliness, the awful, awful loneliness and the sound of silence around the house; the empty rooms, except for the clutter, Annette was always on to me about the clutter, my clutter, which I was always promising her I would clear up "tomorrow" but now it doesn't matter anymore, I'm free to do it whenever I like. The words of a song keep coming to mind, "freedom's just another word for nothing left to lose." How true those words are now. When you lose your lover, your soul mate, your other half, then you truly have nothing left to lose. All that made life worth living is gone. Things which once were thought important are not anymore. Suddenly you can see the true worth of every material thing you ever owned and valued – zilch!

Every day you are haunted by the silence and the space you now have to occupy alone. There is a "sound of silence"; a buzz that constantly fills your head from ear to ear in the absence of any human sound or conversation taking place around you. The empty rooms which once were filled with the joyous sound of Annette's voice and music are now as silent as deep space, and the emptiness only amplifies and gives life to that lonely sound of silence. But the cruellest reminder of what has been lost is the empty bed, the big, smelly, empty bed. That is a constant and painful reminder of my loss. A space we once filled with sensual joy and pleasure is now a crumpled sad reminder of yesterday's passion.

I haven't changed the sheets since Annette passed away three months ago. That's all I have left of her now, her smell, our smell, on the bed we had breakfast in every morning, we talked in, laughed in, argued in, made love in. **But now all I have is the smell of our spent passion.** And I want to keep that for as long as I possibly can, otherwise I may be overcome by the barely controlled and concealed panic that fills my mind, that fills my very being, when I realise that I will never see Annette again this side of the grave. That I will not hold her again, that I will not feel the softness of her body as I hold her tight to me, absorb her body heat into me as we make love, kiss her warm lips, or even just gaze at her as she lies sleeping beside me. All I have of her now is her smell, and I will keep and love that smell as much as I loved Annette herself for as long as I live

She is still alive in her smell.

CHAPTER ONE

Annette passed away on the 14th April, 2009, after a three-month long battle with cancer.

The years were good to Annette; she looked fabulous right up to her untimely passing. She was sixty-two but could have passed for late 40s. We were together almost forty-four years, forty-one of which we were married. We had three children, David, Gina and Robert, and three grandchildren, Senan, Ella-May and Mina.

Forty-four years is a long time to spend with one person, but the years truly did fly by. I would have happily spent four hundred and forty-four more years with Annette. I never contemplated us parting. In saying that I'm not implying that everything in the garden was always rosy. Two normal people cannot spend a lifetime together and not encounter problems along the way, and so it was with Annette and me. We had our moments, but through everything that happened, serious and not so serious, the cement that bound us together was the passion with which we loved each other. It was the sheer physical attraction, the enjoyment and pleasure we gave each other in our love making. This physical attraction was something that was there for me right from the start of our relationship. Though I hasten to add at this point that we were both virgins when we married in 1968, thanks to Annette's control of me mostly.

Looking back on things now I'm glad she kept me in check. The sex, when it did happen, was better for the restraint we showed before marriage and it got better with every passing year. It's what I miss so much now, and of which the big smelly bed is a constant reminder. A reminder of good times, of joyful times, of passionate times, times of warm embraces and long lingering kisses, of two bodies clinging together so not an ounce of the love they shared could escape. The bed is a reminder of arguments and making up, of fun and laughter, and a lifetime of lovemaking now at an end. A reminder that all that's left to me now is a lifetime, or whatever is left of it, of climbing into a cold bed each night and staring at the space for so long filled by Annette, of reaching over to that space to embrace just one more time, the beautiful body that is no longer there, and the pain and tears that go with the now empty bed.

I'm not looking forward to the rest of what I hope will not be a long life, the lonely years that stretch ahead of me are years I do not want. If I sound lacking in gratitude for the life I now have it's because I feel I, we, have been cheated of what could have been, cheated of what our life together could have been in our latter years, the years we should have grown old together and enjoyed our grandchildren as they grew into young adults and our children as they entered their middle years. It should have been a time for reflecting and giving thanks for the life we were fortunate to share. And for Annette it should have been a time to give free reign to the creativity she never had time to fully let flow.

These years should have been our golden years. There will be no gold in them for me now, just years of reflecting on what might have been. Without Annette by my side, life has very little meaning or attraction for me now. All I can see ahead of me is a life of killing time.

****

I composed a poem for Annette's memorial card which started: 'Our journey began on a warm August day, the sky was blue not a trace of grey" and so it was that sunny Sunday, August 1st 1965, when I first set eyes on Annette Kennedy. She was a very beautiful slim, 18-year-old-girl, with greenie/brown eyes and long luxuriant auburn hair. She was in the company of her friend Mary Dunne, and I was with my friend Dennis Molphy and the setting was the foot of Bray Head.

I had not wanted to go to Bray at all that day. I would have much preferred to go to Dalymount Park to see Bohemians play Stoke City, the big attraction being the great Stanley Matthews was playing for Stoke. But Dennis's will prevailed and we ended up getting the train to Bray. When in Bray we did what all lads of twenty have a sworn duty to do – we sized up the female talent on the stony beach.

After a bit of very careful beach-combing we found ourselves in the company of two young ladies. We stayed with them for a time, talking and so forth and then one of us, and after all this time I really don't know who, wanted to disengage, so we made some excuse and left.

We rambled around the beach area for a while and soon noticed that our two lady friends were always close behind us. As we did not want to resume the friendship and the two girls seemed to be tracking our every move, we decided that the only way to get rid of them was to pick up some other female company in the hope that they would get the message.

We made our way from the beach towards Bray Head, with our "tail" behind us all the way. As we started the ascent of the Head I noticed two attractive young ladies sitting on the grass to our left looking in our direction. That was all the encouragement I needed, as I had, as the song goes: "saw what I liked and I liked what I saw, and I said to myself, that's for me."

I immediately made some comment, probably something silly and embarrassing, to the two girls, but as they did not shoo us away we sat down beside them. As we sat talking to Annette and Mary we were glad to notice the other two girls making their way back towards the beach, probably thinking: 'we can do better than them two anyway.'

Thus came about the meeting of Annette Kennedy and Andy Halpin.

We sat talking for a while on the grass and somehow the conversation got around to golf. As there was then a pitch and putt course close by we invited the girls for a game.

When Annette stood up I was hooked. She was wearing dark slacks and a blue blouse-type top. They showed off her slim figure to perfection and it was far from obvious that she was only recently out of hospital having been treated for Anaemia. From there on I stuck to her like glue. I didn't know which one

Dennis fancied, but I was not going to let him get anywhere near Annette. I made it quite clear by my attention to Annette who I fancied and that I was staying with her.

After the game of pitch and putt, which I discovered Annette was not exactly an expert at, we went to the nearby cafe for coffee and ice cream, again I probably monopolised Annette and was not too concerned about how Dennis and Mary were getting on. It was evening by then and we decided to head back to the city before the trains got too packed. We made our way to the station and managed to get a train back to Dublin easily enough.

I did not want the day to end so I suggested we have something to eat and then maybe go to a film. I'm not too sure that Dennis was keen on this, but as I had gone to Bray with him I felt it only fair that he should fall in with my suggestion. We went to the Wimpy Bar on the quays for coffee and chips – class or what!

After more conversation in the café the girls agreed to go to the pictures with us. *Von Ryan's Express* had just opened in the Capitol Cinema and I was a big fan of Frank Sinatra so I said I'd run over and see if I could get some seats for that night's show, I got them, two at either side of the auditorium.

We parted at the entrance saying we would meet again when the show was over. Frank Sinatra was, and still is a firm favourite of mine so I was very glad to see Annette enjoying the film so much. I was a perfect gentleman during the film and did not make any attempt to get over familiar with her. I was just happy to be sitting with such a beautiful girl.

After the show we met up with Dennis and Mary, but before we did I had asked Annette out on another date the following Wednesday which she agreed to. As it was now late we said our goodnight's outside the Capitol. Annette and Mary had to catch a bus to Ballyfermot and Dennis likewise to Finglas. I lived in the city and could walk home.

When the girls left us I told Dennis that I had asked Annette out again, but he said he had not asked Mary on another date. With that knowledge I was now not so sure that Annette would turn up on Wednesday. You know how it is with girls, they like to hunt in packs, even packs of two.

Wednesday came around and off I went in my silver-grey mohair suit and 'Beatles' boots to meet Annette at the 78 bus stop on Aston Quay, facing what was then McBirneys. I had tickets for a Jack Cruise show at the Olympia Theatre. The show started at 8 o clock and Annette was due at 7.30 p.m. so we had plenty of time, or so I thought. The evening turned out to be my introduction to Annette's concept of time, or rather her lack of concept of time. I was there by 7.20 p.m. I did not want to leave her standing around should she be early. I need not have worried, 8 o'clock came and went with no sign of Annette.

I was mortified, I had told my friends that I had a date with this great looking girl, but now it looked like she was going to stand me up. I looked at my watch, 8.10 p.m., what should I do? Keep waiting or accept she was not going to show up and go home and lick my wounds? Five more minutes I decided and that was it, smashing looking bird or not I was not waiting any longer. Just as I was accepting she was not coming, a 78 pulled in and off stepped Annette, all smiles and looking great. What could I say?

She asked me where we were going and I told her I had tickets for a show on the Olympia which started at 8 o'clock and it was now almost 8:15 p.m. She looked at me and said something I was to hear many times in the future: "that's alright; sure it might not start on time."

Naturally the show had started by the time we reached the Olympia, but not to worry at least she had turned up. During the show I was afraid that this might be my first and last date with Annette. Like *Fawlty Towers* in years to come, I had only to see Jack Cruise do his John Joe Mahockey character and I went into kinks of uncontrolled laughter. I'm afraid Cruise was on top form that night with the result that I sat beside Annette with tears of laughter running down my cheeks. Every now and then I could see Annette giving me one of the sideways' looks that I would get to know so well in later life. But back then I was sure she was thinking I was stone mad.

The show ran late and we did not have much time together after it ended. Annette had to catch her bus so I walked her to the bus stop on the quays and asked her for another date. This time I said I would go out to Ballyer so she would not have to rush for a bus, though rush for a bus I learned over the years is the last thing Annette would ever do. I think we made the date for Saturday night. She told me to get off the bus at the Gala Cinema and she would meet me there.

Over the next few weeks, we spent our first few dates going to the cinema. Back then young people did not frequent the pubs as much as now and anyway Annette did not drink and I hardly drank at all then either.

Our first kiss happened on our third time together. I had not dared touch Annette when we went to the Capitol and there was no time after the Olympia. But on our third date in the Gala in Ballyfermot I took my courage into my hands. I slipped my arm around Annette's shoulder in the darkness of the cinema, she did not shy away from my touch so I relaxed a bit and gently caressed her shoulder and the soft flesh on the top of her exposed arm. That's as far as it went.

After the film, we walked up Le Fanu Road to Annette's house. We stopped at the corner and talked for a while. Most of what we said I forget now, but I do know that I asked Annette if she would like to come to a dress dance with me a few weeks later. Years afterwards, Annette told me she was surprised I had asked her to commit to something so far ahead as she was not sure at that point whether she wanted to continue the relationship. After asking me about the dance Annette eventually agreed to go with me. By then it was time for me to run to catch the last bus back to town. I knew by this time where Annette worked so I said I would meet her at the gate of O'Dea's in Wolfe Tone Street on Wednesday for our next date. I then held tight to her shoulders and planted a quick, a very quick, kiss onto her surprised lips.   Then I ran for my bus.

As I ran down Le Fanu Road I was wondering should I have kissed Annette quite so casually, would she think I was not attracted to her by my manner, was I too casual or should I have been more demonstrative? As I thought about it on the way home I decided that on our next date I would take my time and get closer to her when I kissed her goodnight. When our relationship developed and we spoke about its beginnings Annette told me she was pleasantly surprised by that first kiss. And it seems it was not quite as quick as I had thought.

Chapter Two

In the weeks coming up to the dress dance, which was being run by the Karate or Tae Kwando club my friend Dennis and his brother were members of I introduced Annette to my other good friend, Jimmy Morley who was also going to the dress dance with the girl he had recently started going out with Gretta Russell, the girl who was to become his future wife and who would die very young. I did not know it then, but Jimmy and Annette had met before, though neither of them recognised each other. Before coming to Dublin when she was 15, Annette used to work in an ice cream parlour in Newbridge County Kildare. She worked there after school and during her school holidays. Her father worked in Newbridge Cutlery as a saw doctor at that time. Jimmy and myself were members of St. Saviours Football Club, which was run by the Dominican priests from Dominick Street. They used to take some of the boys from the club to the Dominican College in Newbridge for a few days holiday in the summer. I never went on any of these trips, though I remembered the lads talking about an ice cream parlour they used to frequent in the town. They got ice cream highballs which were served by a good looking young girl. The young girl was Annette. It was much later in our relationship I learned about the Newbridge connection.

Before the dance, Dennis had resumed his relationship with his future wife, Rosaleen Prunty, so the three of us were going. with our future life partners, though we did not know that at the time.

In the run up to the dress dance, which at that time was quite a big social occasion and none of us had ever been to one before, I met Annette's parents and family and likewise she met mine. Annette met my parents first. On our fourth date together, the night I met Annette at O'Dea's, I had told my mother I would be bringing her up for tea. I did not tell Annette until I met her that evening. Naturally she did not want to come. I was such a "thick" back then, arranging a big event like that without consulting Annette first. I'm very lucky she stayed with me. Back then I was gormless and naive and not aware of the right thing to do. Anyway Annette did come up to Dominick Street Flats where I lived and I introduced her to my mother and father, my brother Joe came in later and also met Annette.

That first meeting between Annette and my mother turned out to be one of the most embarrassing things that ever happened to me. After we had had our tea my mother took Annette upstairs, on the pretext of showing her the rest of the flat. From what Annette told me later my mother quizzed her extensively on all aspects of her life while I waited and waited and waited downstairs wondering just what was going on. Eventually they came down and we got to leave. Annette let me know she was not too pleased with her first encounter with her future mother-in-law. All I can say is that Annette was the first and only girl I had ever brought to meet my parents, that's not to say I had been with many girls before Annette; I hadn't. I had had a "girlfriend" when I was 15, when we lived in Wellington Street but Annette was the first girl I had ever gone out with more than once. She was the first girl I had ever wanted to go out with more than once, so my mother must have thought I had serious intentions but she did not trust my ability to make the right choice in choosing a 'nice' girlfriend. Even today, all these years later, I cringe when I think of that evening. Incidentally my father was much taken by Annette and never stopped admiring and talking about her "lovely long, dark hair." In years to come, when Annette did cut her hair he was very disappointed, and he never stopped telling her she should not have done it.

My meeting with Annette's parents was more casual than her introduction to mine. It was a Sunday night and we had been out for a walk in Chapelizod. We had gone into a pub for an orange drink and Annette also had a cigarette, she smoked then but not very much. I may have had a glass of Smithwicks,they were simple times then and we were easily pleased. Anyway we made our way back to Annette's house and by this stage I had summoned up the courage to have a "court".

We were "courting" on Annette's doorstep when who should come upon us but her parents, Mary and Bill. They were coming home from their night out in Young's bar down the road. Embarrassment all round. But they made little of it and Bill says to Annette, "Why don't you invite your young man in?"

Annette remained silent so I said something about having to go, as I had a bus to catch. Whereupon Bill says, "sure you have time for a cup of tea." He stepped into the house, leaving a silent Annette and me on the doorstep.

I stood still, not making a move and looked at Annette who I thought, rather reluctantly said, "come on in."

In we went and I was told to sit on the couch, which I did, while Annette went into the kitchen. As I sat down I heard footsteps on the stairs. The door burst open as Annette's two younger sisters, Louise and Caroline, ran into the room. They stopped in their tracks at the sight of a stranger sitting on the couch. Bill came out of the kitchen with a packet of King Crisps for each of them. He told them that I was Annette's "new" boyfriend. After formal introductions, a cup of tea and some toast, I made ready to leave, but just before I could go Annette's brother Liam arrived home. There were more introductions and final goodbyes.

The courting mood of earlier had been broken so our farewell kiss was a tame affair. I said I'd see Annette on Wednesday and ran down the road for the last bus. It took me as far as Conynghan Road and then I had a walk down the quays and home through an almost deserted O'Connell Street. Incidentally, a year or so later I was probably one of the last people apart from the bombers, to see Nelson's Pillar in all its glory. I walked up O'Connell Street and passed the famous landmark on my way home from a date with Annette. It was at about 1.30 a.m. on the night it was blown up.

We had a few more dates before the dress dance. Our dating had now developed a pattern. Annette went to the Miraculous medal devotions on Monday nights as she was a member of the Legion of Mary in Ballyfermot. As a member of the Legion of Mary she visited the sick and old on a Tuesday night and she had a presidium meeting of her guild on Thursday night. A few weeks into our relationship Annette told me she was also studying to go to Brazil as a member of a Legion of Mary offshoot, Viatorus Christi, for which she had to attend meetings on some Friday nights. That only left Wednesday, Saturday and Sunday when we could meet. In order to see more of Annette I used to go to the Miraculous medal devotions with her on Monday night – what a fella will do for love!

After the devotions, if the weather was fine, we sometimes went for a walk and we would maybe stop into Young's pub for an orange and Annette would have a smoke. If the weather was bad we usually went back to Annette's house or occasionally to the Gala. It was during this time that I got an insight into how special a person Annette was and how unselfish she was with her time. I learnt about her concern for people and her desire to help, especially those whom she felt to be marginalised or excluded, where and whenever she could. I did not relish the idea of her going to Brazil, especially as she often spoke about a fellow who was also going and of whom she seemed to be very fond. After a very short time I realized that I was in love with Annette. I wanted to spend the rest of my life with her, but I was not ready to tell her that just yet as I was pretty sure she did not feel the same way about me if she was still talking about going to Brazil.

After a few weeks dating, Annette also informed me that every few Saturday nights she babysat for friends of hers, Frank Lynch, with whom she worked and his wife, Marie. Rather than not see Annette on those Saturday nights I went babysitting with her too. And I must say here and now that I got to enjoy those babysitting sessions very much. When the children went to bed, and I recollect them going early, we had the house to ourselves and we used that time to perfect our kissing and courting technique. So may I say to Frank and Marie all these years later, thanks for the use of your house, it was much appreciated at the time.

I remember on one particular night Frank and Marie were very late coming home which caused me to miss the last bus. Frank gave me a loan of his bike so I could get home. After seeing Annette home, I proceeded to cycle back to town on a bike with no light. It was about 2 o clock in the morning. I got as far as Capel Street when I was stopped by a Garda van containing a couple of gardaí. In my opinion they were anxious to get back to the station for a cup of tea and I became their ticket. I was quizzed about the ownership of the bike and the fact that it had no light. My explanation was not accepted, in spite of the fact that I was willing to bring them to where I lived. It was only up the road in Dominick Street. They could verify my address and issue a summons for no light on the bike. All my pleading was in vain and me and the bike were bundled into the van and brought to the Bridewell. I was locked into a cell for about three or four hours. At 6.00 a.m. or there about the cell was opened and I was told to get my bike and go home. I had survived my one and only night behind bars, all for the sake of love.

CHAPTER THREE

Time moved on and soon it was the day of the dress dance. In the days leading up to it there was great excitement in Annette's house. She was trying on dresses and different hairstyles which caused great excitement with her young sisters and her mother. She told me later it was like preparing for a wedding, with clothes and make-up everywhere. Things were easier for me, all I had to do was hire a dress suit and dickie bow and show up on time.

The night of the dance finally arrived. It was held in the now long gone Metropole Ballroom on O'Connell Street. Dennis and Rosaleen, if I remember correctly, made their own way there, but Jimmy had recently bought a car and after picking up Gretta from Cabra, he picked me up and we all went to Ballyfermot and collected Annette. It was the custom that when a fellow asked a girl to a dress dance and he called to collect her, that he presented her with a large box of chocolates. That's exactly what I did, a large box of Black Magic. She tucked the chocolates under her arm as her young sisters looked on enviously. But Annette promised to keep some for them when she came home. She looked regal as I took her hand and led her to the waiting car.

Back then parking was allowed in the middle of O'Connell Street, which we did and walked over to the Metropole and joined the throngs of other young couples as they made their way into the lush foyer, through crowds of onlookers. Annette looked amazing that night, it was the first of the many times over our years together that I saw how fabulous Annette could look when she dressed for formal occasions. She had a sense of style that was all her own, no one could come near her. She had the ability to make the cheapest dress look like a priceless designer creation and that was before the term "designer dress" had been coined. Although all the girls were wearing long white dresses that night, to my eyes Annette outshone them all in her figure-hugging silk dress with her hair in a beehive style, high on her head. It made her look so tall, slim and elegant. If I had not loved her before, I could not but have fallen in love with her that night. She was like a film star on Oscar night.

We danced a lot that night to the music of Joe Coughlan and the Metropole orchestra, with vocalist Pat Montana. Annette loved to dance but I'm afraid my dancing left a lot to be desired, except for the slow numbers, when I held Annette tight and let the music carry us around the floor. I did a lot of that on the night. The night was a great success and we quite literally did not want it to end. Thinking back on it I don't think we drank alcohol at all, we were content with soft drinks, and probably enjoyed the night all the more for that. How different things are now.

The three girls met each other for the first time that night and seemed to get on very well together, which added to the enjoyment. After the dance myself and Annette, high on the excitement of the night got a taxi back to Ballyfermot. For the first time I stayed in Annette's overnight. On the couch in the front room I hasten to add.

Our dating habits changed after the dress dance. Before that night we mostly went to the pictures, but now we started going to dances, which Annette preferred. I could hardly put one foot in front of the other whereas Annette was a good dancer. She was very patient with me and worked hard at getting me to jive, a dance she loved to do. In the beginning dancing was an ordeal for me. I wasn't any good at it and, worst of all, I felt embarrassed on the floor as I believed everyone was looking at my clumsy attempts. But I also knew that if I wanted to continue dating Annette I had to be prepared to bring her to dances. After a while, with her help, I became a not good but adequate dancer and I started to enjoy going to dances which we did quite often. The Metropole, Clerys, The National, The Ierne, The Crystal, The TV Club and occasionally The Portmarnock Country Club became the backdrop to our developing romance.

All of a sudden our first Christmas together was ahead of us and our relationship seemed to be going from good to very good. We were very loving and affectionate towards each other indeed I sometimes found it hard not to stray beyond what Annette considered acceptable behaviour, but she was always gentle in a controlling way in that department. She said to me years later when we were married, and if I had known it at the time I might have pressed her just a little bit harder, that she sometimes wanted to go further, but knew one of us had to be strong. Don't you just love strong women!

I still had not mentioned the love word to Annette, though I think she had a good idea how I felt about her and I was beginning to believe she had, ------ how shall I put it, fond feelings for me. Also she had been in the flat in Dominick Street on quite a few occasions since that embarrassing first visit and relations between her and my mother had improved considerably. As a matter of fact my mother, indeed both my parents had become very fond of Annette.

I gave Annette an electric hair dryer as a Christmas present and she gave me a jumper that first year. On Christmas Eve, after spending the day together in town, we went back to the Wimpy Bar on the Quays and had a slap-up mixed grill before I left her to the last bus from town at 9 o'clock. We both stayed in our own homes on Christmas Day and I went out to Ballyer on Stephen's Day. I ingratiated myself with her parents and family by bringing presents, small ones, for all.

Christmas 1965 was good for our relationship, we visited each other's family and got on well with them. We got to know each other better in the relaxed holiday atmosphere. I think that just maybe it was the time Annette started to think twice about going to Brazil. We went to a few dances over the Christmas period as well and spent New Year's Eve in Annette's house at a family party sing-song. It was the first of many such occasions, and it was family sing-songs which would cause friction between Annette and me over the years. Coming from a small family, I only had one brother, I always found these family get-togethers a bit boring, and the idea of singing in front of people was always a source of embarrassment to me. I tried to avoid going whenever possible, and this evasiveness annoyed Annette.

She loved meeting her family and socialising with her sisters as they got older. Over the years this was one of the things that we, from time to time, crossed swords over.

Chapter Four

Our romance went from strength to strength over the next year or so. Annette spoke less and less about going to Brazil, although she had not entirely given up on the idea. She still went to the Friday night meetings from time to time.

We were now both quite comfortable with each other and with each other's families, my mother and Annette were getting on like a house on fire and were laying the foundations for their future relationship. We had also started to go out as a foursome now and again with Annette's friends, Lillian Long and her boyfriend Colm Montgomery. On a number of occasions we went out to the Embankment in Tallaght, then owned by the legendary Mick McCarthy. We didn't know then that on the way we were passing the very spot we would in the future live in for over 30 years. On one famous occasion, after a night of drinking, we missed the last bus from the Embankment. In the depths of winter; with snow on the ground, we walked past what in a few years became Raheen Green, where we would live most of our married life together. It was just an empty field then, and we had to continue on walking past Tallaght Village before we could get a taxi. We liked to go to places that were a little bit different and out of the way. During that phase of our courtship we also went to the Blue Gardenia in Brittas a number of times. It's funny now looking back on those times but we seemed to be drawn to that part of Dublin. Maybe it was not so strange that we bought a house out in Tallaght and lived happily there for over 30 years.

Speaking of the Blue Gardenia I remember a night we spent there before we were married. It was around Christmas time and the "Blue" was decorated accordingly, fairy lights, Christmas tree and lots of tinsel. By this time we had both started to take a drink, vodka and lime for Annette and a pint for me. The night was good, the atmosphere was great and we did not notice the time slipping by. The result was we missed the bus. Back in those days there were very few taxis to be got outside the city limits. No housing estates had yet been built out in west Dublin so there was no need for taxis to be around. We came out of the pub and through innocence, stupidity or more probably too much to drink we stood at the bus stop thinking that just maybe a bus would come. We were hardy creatures back then, I only had a suit on and Annette was wearing a light dress and coat. The ground was covered in snow and as we stood under the light beside the bus stop it began to fall again. The scene was so romantic, two young lovers wrapped around each other in a lamp lit snow scene, the only trouble was we were freezing and in danger of being frozen together like two statues. We must have stood there for the best part of an hour before a passing motorist, one of the very few on the road that night, took pity on us and picked us up. They dropped us back to civilisation, where we got a taxi to Ballyfermot.

Another place that became a favourite of ours was the Shangri-La restaurant in Bullock Harbour, Dalkey. The Shangri-La was a beautiful little place reminiscent of "Rick's Bar" in *Casablanca*. For ten shillings and six pence you could get a meal and dance the night away to a three-piece combo. We loved it and when we became engaged it's where we celebrated the occasion.

And so our romance developed, we both liked the same things, going to the same places, being with the same kind of people, but, most of all, we were only completely happy when we were in each other's company, and we were content with that, as long as we could be together we were happy. As I said earlier, we were both virgins when we married, that was because Annette wanted it that way, but in all honesty sex was not an issue with us. Oh sure on a number of occasions I would have gone further if I had been let, but really, it did not impinge on our relationship at all. I was more than happy just to be in Annette's company. The sex when it did happen after we were married was great, Annette gave herself unreservedly and as we were both learning we could laugh at our first clumsy but loving attempts at love making. I do believe now that not having sex before we were married contributed a great deal to the successful and long marriage we went on to have. If we had given in to our (my!) desires before marriage I think there would have been a lot less fun on our honeymoon. We would have been used to having a sex life and nothing would have been new and experienced together for the first time as man and wife. By waiting until we were married I believe we laid the foundations of trust and love, the ingredients that are so necessary in a marriage for the years that follow the honeymoon. We could look at each other on our honeymoon and know we were both giving each other something we had reserved for each other from the moment we vowed to love no one else for the rest of our lives. And so it was with Annette and me.

CHAPTER FIVE

For the times that were in it, we both had reasonably good jobs. I was working as a store man with an electrical goods company, Neasden Distributors in Essex Street and Annette was a fully qualified upholsteress with O'Dea's the mattress makers. If we had wanted to we were in a better position than many to make plans for the future. I had by this time told Annette how I felt about her, albeit in a rather clumsy way as we sheltered from the rain under a tree near Bohernabreena, and I was thinking of our future together. But Annette, although she was very fond of me was not ready to commit to a future together just yet.

Our relationship had settled down to a comfortable routine, Miraculous medal on Monday night, the Gala or somewhere in town on Wednesday night and a dance, with the occasional baby-sitting gig, on Saturday nights. Life was good, but I was pushing Annette a bit on our future. She still had not fully given up the idea of Brazil though I thought it was fading a bit. But I knew enough about Annette by this time to know that the final decision on that would have to be her own choice. If I pushed too hard I knew I might just tip the scales in favour of Brazil. So I had to be careful how I went about it.

During the latter part of 1966, we had a few little rows probably brought on by the uncertainty of the situation. On one occasion we actually broke up for a short time, a very short time. We had had an argument about something or other on the Saturday night and Annette said maybe it was time for a break. She'd taken me by surprise, but not wanting to let her know that, I said something like "that's fine by me" and went home. By Wednesday I was on the phone to Annette in O'Dea's ready to apologise for whatever it was I had done or said to upset her, and plead with her to come back. But I didn't have to. I knew by her tone when she answered the phone that she was as broke up about it as I was, so I just apologised for whatever I may have said on Saturday and she did likewise. We resumed where we had left off later that night with an evening of kiss and make up in the darkness of the Gala.

I felt it was now make or break time with us. One night, as we walked up Le Fanu Road, coming home from a date, I plucked up the courage and asked Annette to marry me. Annette remembers it somewhat differently, she says I did not ask her to marry me, but rather said: "I want to marry you." At this stage I don't know what I said or whose memory is right, but I was not expecting Annette to be surprised when I asked, or told her I wanted to marry her. I had, I thought, made it perfectly clear how I felt about her, so the next logical step in my opinion was an engagement and marriage. As you may have guessed Annette did not give me an answer there and then, but she did not say no. I let the matter rest and did not press Annette on the issue. We continued to see each other every Monday, Wednesday and Saturday.

Soon Christmas 1966 was upon us. In many ways it was a repeat of the previous year, an exchange of presents and visits to each other's families. The one thing different was I asked Annette if she would like to become engaged, and this time she said yes.

We decided to get engaged the following Easter. We did not say anything to anyone about our impending engagement for a while. Annette, being the daughter she was, wanted me to formally ask her father for her hand in marriage first. I got on well with Bill, Annette's father, and liked him a lot. He was a very nice quiet man and not someone to be intimidated by, nevertheless I was not looking forward to asking him for Annette's hand in marriage. I put it off for as long as I could.

We started saving hard about this time as we wanted to have somewhere of our own to live after we got married. We eased off on the amount of money we spent on dates. I took on a part-time job, a football pools round, to earn more money and Annette took overtime whenever she could get it. The housing situation was bad at that time and there was no chance of us getting any kind of council or corporation housing. We knew that if we did not want to end up with either of our parents, a situation we never envisaged anyway, we would have to buy a house of our own.

Shortly after Christmas we heard about a new housing co-op which was being formed by a journalist named Joe McAnthony. We found out more about it and on a wet miserable Monday night we and a few hundred other couples anxious to secure their own home, queued for two hours at a basement office in Blessington Street. We put our names on a list in the hope that someday we would be able to buy our own home.

This was also the day we went public with the news of our engagement. After queuing for hours in the rain in Blessington Street, we looked like two drenched down and outs and after at last getting our names on the list, we went back to Dominick Street. When my mother opened the door and saw us standing on the balcony, with the rain running down our faces and necks and squelching out of our shoes she just stood staring at us with an amazed look on her face.

"What in the name of God happened to you; where have you been?" she exclaimed as she ushered us into the flat.

Standing before her, like two street urchins, and with my father looking equally amazed and puzzled sitting on a chair behind her, I blurted out: "we're getting engaged and we have been putting our names down on a list for a house."

All my parents could do was look at us in a state of complete incomprehension. Without referring to the engagement, as if it had not been mentioned, my mother said "get those wet clothes off you before you both get your death of cold" but the secret was out - Annette and Andy were getting engaged.

In honesty I don't think anyone was surprised. But it meant I now had no choice, I had to start practicing my formal request to Annette's father to ask for her hand in marriage. Annette took pleasure in my predicament and ribbed me about my task. She kept saying I would have to go down on my knees to beg her father for her hand, and he just might refuse.

A week later the terrible moment came. It was a Sunday night, a night I normally did not see Annette, but for some reason she wanted me to ask on this particular night. I went out to Ballyfermot but when I got there Bill and Mary had already gone down to Young's. We sat in with Annette's young sisters, Louise, Claire and Caroline, talking, playing, and looking at the TV. Eventually Annette sent her sisters to bed and we sat waiting for her parents to return. They did shortly after ten. After a bit of small talk Mary called Annette into the kitchen, leaving myself and Bill alone in the front room. I don't know which of us was the most nervous, but at least Bill had a few pints in him to fortify him for our joint ordeal. After what seemed like an eternity of silence between us, I cleared my throat and blurted out something like: "hem, ehh I, I, ehh, Annette and I would like to get married and Annette said I should ask you first, is it alright if we get married?" Bill just looked at me and said "ah yea that's alright" and it was done and dusted. The things women put men through.

Mary and Annette then came out of the kitchen looking expectantly at both of us. I took Annette's hand and said "it's all right he said yes." But Mary was not as easily placated, "did we have somewhere to live" she wanted to know. We told her we had no intention of moving in with her and that we had joined the housing co-op and would be buying our own house. After a little bit more conversation about our plans and when exactly we were getting engaged, a few bottles of beer were produced. They were consumed by myself and Bill. After that I took my leave of my future in-laws and said a very relieved good night to Annette in the hall.

Chapter Six

It was full steam ahead to our engagement. We had decided it would be at Easter 1967, with the hope that we would be able to get married sometime the following year. 1967 was also the year Annette reached the age of 21, her birthday being the 13th of August, so heavy expenditure was envisaged in the near future.

We continued to save all we could and kept in touch with the housing co-op but after a while it became obvious that we were not going to get a house from that quarter anytime soon, certainly not in the timeframe we had set for our engagement and wedding. But we did not let that upset us too much and continued to make plans for our future.

We got engaged on Easter Saturday, 25th of March, 1967. My brother Joe worked as a jeweller and he was able to get us a note of introduction to a firm of jewellery wholesalers in Grafton Street, and on a beautiful sunny and warm Easter Saturday morning, I met Annette at McBirneys. She looked absolutely stunning in a blue and white high-necked flower print dress which was cut away at the shoulders revealing her smooth, tanned arms. Her hair was long, loose, and cascading over her shoulders. She carried a white bag and a light white cardigan, a white silk-type scarf and black court shoes. (Annette's just told me the type of shoe she was wearing that day.) I wore a dark blue suit.

After taking her in my arms and kissing her, we set off up Grafton Street to the wholesalers to choose an engagement ring. Annette did not take long to decide on the ring she wanted. After looking at a few trays of diamond engagement rings, she held up a diamond solitaire set in platinum on a gold band. She'd decided that it was the one she wanted. I had about £150 in my pocket, some of it savings we had withdrawn and a small loan I had taken out to cover the day's expenses. I had no idea how much the ring would cost and it only then dawned on me that I might just not have enough. I waited nervously as the assistant took the note of introduction from us and went into a small partitioned area off the showroom. He came back in a few moments with the ring in a small box wrapped in silver paper. As he handed the box to Annette he said to me: "that ring would normally cost £200, but with discounts and because we know Joe, it will cost you £75". Phew, with a huge sense of relief I took the money from my pocket, gave him £80 pounds and told him to keep the change.

We left the showrooms and went over to Robert Roberts Cafe for coffee and cakes. Annette opened the box and I put the ring on her finger. After our coffee and cakes we got the bus to Dalkey and spent the afternoon there as we had booked a table in the Shangri-La for that night. I vaguely remember us having a drink in a pub in Dalkey before going to the restaurant, but I am not absolutely sure of that, as I may be mixing it up with another occasion, also I was intoxicated by the events of the day and how beautiful Annette looked.

As the evening set in we made our way to the Shangri -La on Bullock Harbour, got our candlelit table for two and danced until midnight. Shortly after I had put the ring on Annette's finger she'd taken it off and put it into her bag. When we were in the Shangri-La she took it out and gave it to me to so I could put it on her finger again and formally become engaged.

We got talking to a more mature (40s) couple in the restaurant who had noticed our romantic behaviour and guessed we were celebrating something or other. They insisted on giving us a lift back to the city at the end of the night. The couple dropped us on Stephen's Green and we got a taxi back to Ballyfermot where Bill and Mary were waiting up for us so they could see the ring. Needless to say I did not go home that night but slept on the couch in the front room, engagement or no engagement things didn't change on that score.

We had no big celebration for our engagement, but the following Sunday, as a means of introducing our parents to each other and with the permission of my parents, I invited Bill and Mary down to Dominick Street for a meal and a few drinks.

The day went very well and both sets of parents got on well together. During the course of the evening it was discovered that my father and Mary had lived very near each other in Queen Street when they were young, many years before. So now, each of us having got the imprimatur of our future in-laws, the engagement was sealed.

1967 was also the year we went on holidays together for the first time, to beautiful sunny Cobh in Cork. When we announced to our families that we were going on holidays together the first reaction we got was silence. Then, a few seconds later when the news had been decoded to fit Ireland of the 1960s, they asked, "are you, and where are you going to stay?" When we said "in a B & B," to borrow a phrase from the present, the elephant in the room was never mentioned, all they said was "oh" and a perfunctory, "well, enjoy yourselves." And as clear and bright as a neon sigh flashing on their heads, we could see the rest of the sentence, "but for God's sake, not too much!"

We stayed in a B & B, at the back of the Cathedral. We had separate rooms, at the insistence of the "bean an tí" as we were not yet married. I jest you not. This was Ireland in the 1960's – dynamic and forward looking and respectful of everybody's point of view and where personal freedom reigned! Annette was lodged with a few girls she did not know and I was stabled with a French guy who drenched himself in cologne. He almost choked me with the amount he splashed on every morning.

Notwithstanding the sleeping arrangements we had a great time, and the weather wasn't too bad either. Being alone with Annette every day and night for a week was a temptation for me. I remember a sunny day on Inchidonney Beach when things got hot, and I'm not referring to the weather, but Annette held firm. Her motto was, "thus far shalt thou go but no further."

The other big event of 1967 was Annette's 21st birthday. Back then a 21st was not the huge occasion for celebrating that it is today and we made no big plans for it. We were still saving for a house, in the hope and expectation we would be getting married the following year. Nevertheless the occasion had to be marked. After the engagement and the holiday I had very little money left apart from what we'd saved, so I faced a dilemma in what I could get Annette for her birthday. I knew Annette would like to go out somewhere on the weekend of her birthday so I booked a table in the Shangri-La for Saturday, 12th August, as her birthday fell on a Sunday.

With that done I set about seeing what I could afford to buy her for a present. I quickly discovered the answer was very little. I loved Annette very much and wanted to give her something special for her 21st but my funds dictated otherwise.

By Friday of that week I still did not have a present for Annette. Panic was setting in, with the money I had at my disposal I could not buy her the type of present she deserved. That night as I was sitting in my bedroom at home playing my Frank Sinatra records a thought occurred to me, I could sell my collection of records and that would get me enough money to buy Annette a very good present. But could I? I had been a fan of Sinatra's for years and had a large collection of LPs, was I willing to sell them all, or most of them to buy a present for a girl? It did not take me long to make up my mind. I listened to my favourites, "Look to your heart" "Songs for swinging lovers" "Only the lonely" and one or two more for the last time, dusted them off, bundled them up and got ready to sell them the next day.

First thing Saturday morning, without telling anyone, I put the records into a large bag. There were about 30 altogether, mostly Sinatra. I headed down to the record shop, I think it was Dolphin Discs in Capel Street, where I had bought many of the records I was now trying to sell. I forget exactly how much I got for them, certainly not nearly as much as I had paid when I bought them new, but I had enough to buy Annette a pretty decent present and to have a good night out as well.

I went straight from the record shop to a jeweller's on O'Connell Street beside the old Metropole cinema, Murphy's I think was the name of the shop. Earlier in the week I had seen what I thought was a very nice Celtic design gold and pearl necklace there that I was sure Annette would like. With all my worldly possessions in my hand I went in and asked the assistant for "the Celtic necklace that was in the window" I handed over my £17, 10 shillings, and the assistant gift wrapped the necklace and handed it to me, winking as he did so. I went out of the shop a happy shopper.

That night we went to the Shangri-La and I gave Annette her present. She was delighted with it, and the following year when we got married she wore it at our wedding and at many subsequent events over the course of our life together. In fact that necklace proved so popular with Annette, her sisters and her friends that many of them got a loan of it over the years. It was worn at many a wedding. The necklace became something of a family heirloom over the years, our daughter Gina now has the necklace that was bought all those years ago with the proceeds of the sale of my Frank Sinatra record collection.

CHAPTER SEVEN

They say true love never runs smooth and I was to discover that fact for myself. Some time after Annette's birthday she broke off the engagement and gave me back the ring, in the middle of Dame Street.

I admit now I deserved it. I was never as outgoing or as sociable as Annette and I was happy just to be in her company. By this time I was seeing very little of my friends Jimmy and Dennis and that was fine by me. But Annette wanted more and she felt she was losing contact with her friends. She wanted us to mix with people more and to not always be on our own. I resisted this as I did not feel comfortable in the company of people I did not know or at least did not know well.

On the night Annette gave me back the ring it was a few days after we had been out with one of her friends and her boyfriend. Annette had said nothing on the night but she now began to lay into me about my behaviour as she saw it when we were last out together. She said I'd acted bored and rude to her friend and her boyfriend, I tried to explain to her that I had nothing in common with the boyfriend and therefore very little to say to him. But Annette had her dander up and she didn't think this was a good enough explanation. Word followed word and possibly some things were said that should have been left unsaid. The end result was that Annette took off the engagement ring and handed it to me saying something like maybe we were not suited to each other, our differences were too great so we should break it off now.

I was shocked. While I knew we had our differences, I was prepared to overlook them because I believed we loved each other enough to overcome and surmount any differences between us. I stood in the street with the ring in my hand, as Annette turned on her heel and headed home. I did not say anything at home about the broken engagement and kept the ring in my pocket. I did not try to contact Annette either as I had done the last time we'd split up. Instead I let things rest for a few days.

So as not to arouse any suspicions about the situation at home, I continued to go out on the nights I would normally be with Annette. I walked the streets thinking about what I would do.

A week passed and I was feeling pretty miserable. I could not go on like this much longer. The other problem was that Annette usually came up to Dominick Street once a week and if she was missing from the scene my mother would start asking questions. I agonised about what I should do, leave well enough alone or contact Annette. But if I did what would be her reaction? While I knew I could not live without Annette, would she have discovered she could get along quite well without me in her life?

After what seemed a life time without Annette I decided I would confront the situation head on. I went and stood outside O'Dea's one night as Annette was knocking off work. I was standing at the old church railings opposite O'Dea's gate when I saw Annette coming up the ramp leading to the street. She was with her friend Lily McHugh when she saw me. As I hesitated to cross the road, Annette said something to Lily. Her friend waved at me and then walked off in the other direction. I started to walk over towards Annette, and as I did I saw a smile develop on her face. I returned an embarrassed smile back. I went over to her, took her hand and gave her a kiss on the lips. Both of us tried to apologise for our behaviour but neither of us wanted to hear the other's apology. We just wanted to forget the whole incident. Annette took back the ring and no more was said.

After that little hiccup I was on my best behaviour and started concentrating on finding us somewhere to live after we were married. By this stage the housing co-op was looking like a non runner. It was encountering major problems securing land at a reasonable price so we started looking elsewhere for accommodation. Even though we were both working and had reasonable jobs, the price of a new house seemed way beyond our means, particularly as we knew the archaic rules that were in place in O'Dea's. Those rules meant that Annette would have to give up her job after we got married. We would be living on one wage until such time as she could get another job. And then if a baby or two came along she would be confined to the home full-time. We continued saving as much as we could and hoped that something would turn up for us.

Despite these handicaps we threw caution to the wind and set the date for our wedding, even though we had no idea at the time where we would be living after the honeymoon. Full of blind romantic optimism we were sure something would turn up, after all wasn't Annette still doing the Miraculous medal novena and both our mothers were burning the feet off their favourite saints with lighted candles. Tuesday September 24th 1968 was the date we set for the wedding, Tuesday because it coincided with our choice of a honeymoon flight to sunny Spain and the church was also available on that day. I think we were the first of all our friends who got married to fly to foreign shores for their honeymoon. Never mind the fact that we could barely afford it.

After the slight interruption before Christmas things were back on course romance wise and I was pretty much falling into line with whatever Annette wanted. Her next request was for us to do a pre marriage course. I was not too keen about it at first but I knew Annette would be very annoyed if I objected. I supposed it was a small price to ask if it helped us to have a successful marriage.

In the spring of 1968, March I think it was, we enrolled at the Dominican Priory Dominick Street. The pre-marriage course was for one evening a week for eight weeks and it was conducted by Fr. Fergal O'Connor. And I must say I enjoyed it. It was not at all what I had expected . Fr. O'Connor was a very liberal minded priest and spoke very frankly, and with a great sense of humour, about marriage and all the things that could go wrong or go right. He said it all depended on the couple's willingness to be tolerant and open-minded in the situations they would be confronted with over the course of their marriage. How right he was.

The eight weeks sped by and I found myself looking forward to Monday night and the talks given by Fr. O'Connor. It was also an opportunity for us to meet and talk to other couples with the same confused expectations and hopes about their future as we had. We found that despite our different backgrounds and social class we were pretty much all the same in the dreams we had for our futures. We all wanted to live happily ever after.

Chapter Eight

It was while we were attending the pre-marriage course that we got news of the chance to buy a house that was within our price range. A work colleague of Annette's had, through a third party been introduced to an agent who was handling the sale of artisan dwellings. He and his wife had recently bought one situated off Thomas Street and he was very pleased with it. Artisan dwellings were old, and, in most cases, single-storey houses in various areas scattered around the city. They had been built originally in the 19th century for tradesmen and craft workers. It was not the most salubrious place to start our marriage but we could afford the house and it would be our own. Annette told me what her friend had said to her and it sounded hopeful. Her friend then invited us up to see his house which was in better condition than I had expected it to be. If we got a house as good I knew we'd be more than happy to start our marriage there.

We got the name of the agent, a Mr. McCauley, from Annette's friend and wasted no time in contacting him. He turned out to be a Donegal man about 60 years of age, with a thick accent and a bad limp, who lived near the North Strand. We made an appointment to see him and went down to his house one night, which was also an Artisan dwelling. It was also in very good condition, and I thought a similar one would be perfect for us. I think he thought we were innocents abroad and he'd seen us coming. He began to lay it on thick about how difficult it was to get an Artisan dwelling. They were in very big demand and people were prepared to pay almost as much for one in a good area as they would for a new house. Not many were coming on the market and when one did come you had to be prepared to outbid others for it, and so he went on.

We sat listening to all this and my heart was sinking. When at last he stopped talking, he looked at us and said, "How much money have you got?" We looked at each other and back at him,

then I said, "A friend of Annette's said he bought one for £1000."
He said, "Well sometimes you can be lucky. I don't
think I could get one now cheaper than £1500."
"I think that would be a bit too much for us," I remember
saying. McCauley then said, "there's one going near here in
need of repair. I might be able to get it for a bit less"

"Can we see it?" I asked.

"Not tonight, I'd have to make arrangements with the
owners. I'll tell you what, come back next week and bring £100
and we'll go and see what can be arranged," McCauley said.

With those words ringing in our ears we walked down to
Dominick Street and told my parents we had the chance of
buying a house. While all this was going on we were continuing
to do the pre-marriage course and make preparations for the
wedding and the honeymoon. We had never been out of the
country before (Annette is reminding me that she was in England
on Legion of Mary work before I met her) so we needed to get
passports. We'd booked the honeymoon through a company
called Global Travel who used to be in business at the bottom
of Grafton Street, 10 days half-board in the Santa Rosa Hotel,
Lloret de Mar on the Costa Brava. The church was also booked
for a 12 0'clock Mass on Tuesday 24th September.

The next step was to decide on a hotel. We'd looked at a
few but Annette's heart was set on a hotel we had become a
bit familiar with through our visits to Dalkey, so we booked
the Khyber Pass Hotel, It was just outside Dalkey village,
overlooking the sea and Dalkey Island. It was a hugely romantic
setting for our big day. The hotel is no longer there. It was a
victim of what became Ireland's passion for apartment block
living in later years. Our wedding was going to be quite a small
affair by today's standard, 52 guests, mostly family and a few
friends.

We went back to Mr McCauley as arranged a week later.
He took us literally around the corner to Clinches Court North
Strand – four single-storey houses facing another line of single-
storey houses, in a narrow lane off the North Strand Road. Our
future home was no. 7. It was a red brick house with a narrow

wooden door and a single window in the front. For a single-storey house it was quite high, with a large upward slanting roof and two chimney pots.

It was hard to know what to make of it from the outside. Let's just say we did not think "this we must have" Mr McCauley knocked on the door and it was opened by a man in his early thirties, in need of a shave. We could also hear the sound of babies crying. We were invited into a small hall area where we were introduced to the unshaven man whose name I now forget. Mr McCauley told him we were interested in buying his house. He may have grunted something, but I forget what. He then said that his wife was feeding the babies in the bedroom which we could tell by the noise on the right side of the hall. He led us through the bedroom which we entered directly from the small hall, trying to ignore his wife feeding the babies, and into a large middle room which contained a couch, a table and a few armchairs. There was also a fire place and the light was on although it was still daylight, the room was in the middle of the house. It had only one small window, to the extreme left hand side of the room which looked out on a very enclosed part of the backyard. The extended wall of the house next door blocked the natural light from the room.

So far so not so good.

We then went into the kitchen which was bright and airy. It contained a kitchen table and chairs, a sink unit, cooker and kitchen cabinet. There was also a large bright window at the back wall. This had been built-on to the original house. There was also a door at the left hand side which led out to the backyard, which is where the toilet was situated. As we'd been touring the house, the wife had finished feeding the children, a baby about a year old and a little girl about three. She said we could now have a look at the bedroom. Not wishing to be too intrusive we just stood at the door between the two rooms to view it. It contained a double bed, a cot, a wardrobe, and a fireplace.

When the viewing had finished, we stood in the hall with Mr. McCauley and he asked us if we were interested. We quite literally did not know what to say. I just looked at Annette and I could see the disappointment in her eyes. Just for something to say I asked how much the house would cost. Mr. McCauley said £1500. I shook my head and said it was too much. We started to leave and McCauley said to wait a minute. He went back into the middle room while we stood in the hall in silence.

A minute or two later McCauley came back and said they would be willing to take £1300 for the house. He also said they would repair the window in the middle room which we had pointed out would not open. Still we hesitated and said we would have to think about it. McCauley left with us and continued to point out the great value the house was and how convenient it was as it was so near the city. He also mentioned the height of the house which we had noticed before we went in. He said that this was because these houses were meant to be two-storey houses but the builder had gone bust while they were being built and did not finish them and we had the option in the future of opening up a large attic space should we require it later on. We said we would think about it and let him know in a few days.

We went home quite disappointed that night as we had built our hopes up on getting a house s like the one Annette's work colleague had bought. When Annette told her friend in work the next day he said he had had to do a lot of work to his house when he first bought it and not to be put off by that. He felt that Artisan houses were a good buy but you had to be prepared to do some work on them. We also spoke to Annette's father, Bill. He was very handy with his hands and he agreed to have a look at it for us.

We contacted Mr. McCauley again and made arrangements to look at the house once more. When we went with Bill it did not seem quite as bad as we had first thought. Bill pointed out a few things about the house that he thought could be improved upon, one being the entrance from the hall through the bedroom and into the middle room. Putting in a narrow corridor from the entrance hall he felt was the answer to this as the bedroom was quite big. He also felt we could move the outside toilet to the side of the middle room, effectively bringing it inside, although this would further reduce the light in the middle room. It was an option we could try if we wanted an inside toilet. He also noticed the height of the house and said an attic was very feasible. So feeling a bit more assured about the house we discussed it again. We knew that with the date for the wedding approaching fast, we had to make a decision. A new house was out at this point, as we were overstretching ourselves with the wedding and honeymoon in Spain so we decided that if we could get the house for about £1ooo we would take it.

We went back to Mr. McCauley and asked if the sellers would accept £1000. He said he would ask but he did not think so. It was all we could afford, as apart from the purchase price there would also be McCauley's fee for finding the house, £100, and solicitor's fees, plus the cost of redecorating and any renovations that had to be carried out. To cut a long story short a price of £1150 was finally agreed. We went to the Building Society for a loan of £1000 which together with what we had managed to save would be just about enough to buy the house, carry out the necessary renovations and cover the fees to McCauley and the solicitors.

Everything seemed to be falling into place. The wedding was set, the honeymoon, hotel and church were booked and now we had our house or so we thought but a hitch developed shortly before the wedding. We got a letter from the building society stating that they had discovered that Clinches Court, and that included our house, was part of a redevelopment plan for Dublin City. The area was due to be demolished in the near future and as a consequence they would not be loaning us the money to buy the house. This news threw all our plans into disarray and we began to panic a bit. Through our solicitors we asked what could be done. They made enquiries and discovered that the redevelopment plans had been on hold for years and nobody knew when exactly they would be starting. With this information we went back to the building society. We pointed out the new information we had received and pleaded for the loan. Eventually, after what seemed like a lifetime, the Building

Society agreed to give us the loan provided we got a guarantee from the City Council that if they redeveloped the area they would compensate us fully for the full market value of the house. Eventually we got this guarantee and got the loan. But things had been delayed so much that there was no possibility of us moving into the house after our honeymoon. Incidentally to this day the area has not been redeveloped and no. 7 Clinches Court is still standing.

Chapter Nine

Our wedding was a rather small affair for two reasons, one being Bill and Mary wanted to pay for it. We were conscious that they were not exactly flush with money, so we decided to keep it to immediate family and some friends. Also we ourselves did not want a big expensive wedding with lots of people we hardly knew at it. It suited us to keep the numbers down and to only invite people we really wanted there. And that's how it was, 52 people we wanted to share our wedding day with.

The day was fine weather wise, a nice warm, sunny September day, soft white puffy clouds drifting through blue skies and not a trace of rain. Very reminiscent of the day we'd met, just over three years before in Bray – the day I won my lotto. It could not have been more perfect. Mother Nature was smiling on us. But then human error intruded.

The wedding was due to be celebrated after 12 o'clock Mass in the Church of the Assumption in Ballyfermot. But as the Angelus struck I was still in Dominick Street. The car booked to take me, my best man my brother Joe, and my parents, to the church failed to turn up. It was supposed to pick us up at about 11.30, drop us at the church and then go and pick up Annette and her father. 11.30 came and went and there was no sign of the car; twenty to twelve came and went, still no sign of the big white car. Remember back then there were no mobile phones and we did not have a phone in the flat. Indeed I don't think anyone in the flats had a phone then so there was no way to contact the car rental company.

At a quarter to twelve I could wait no longer. After taking one last look over the balcony to see if the car was coming I ran down O'Connell Street in my morning suit. I flew into the office of the car company in D'Olier Street to enquire where was my car. They had the time wrong; they thought we wanted the car at 12 o clock in Dominick Street and it was now on its way there, so I had to run back up O'Connell Street. As I entered Granby Lane at the back of the flats the car was there. With great haste and to the cheers of the neighbours we all bundled into the car and headed to Ballyfermot.

In Ballyfermot panic had also set in. Annette's mother and the bridesmaids, her four sisters and her friend Mary Abbey, and her brother Liam had left for the church at a quarter to twelve in the bus we had hired to take the guests to Dalkey, in anticipation of the wedding car arriving soon after to pick Annette and her father up. When they arrived at the church they had expected to see the groom waiting expectantly for his bride, but there was no sign of the groom.

When the 12 o'clock' bells rang out and there was still no sign of the car carrying the groom they began to get nervous. To help calm the evident tension of the waiting guests Annette's mother began a decade of the rosary, to pray for divine intervention so that the groom would turn up.

At approximately 12 15 p.m. their prayers were answered when the white wedding car disgorged an embarrassed groom, best man and their parents, and, without further delay, sped up Le Fanu Road to pick up (according to herself) a completely unperturbed bride. She had no doubt whatsoever her groom would turn up.

After the delay I wasted no time in taking my place at the altar. After a few minutes I was relieved to hear the organist strike up, *Here Comes the Bride*. I kept looking straight ahead at the altar as the music was playing, until from the corner of my eye I could see that Bill was beside me. I then turned to my left, he stepped away and I beheld Annette. She looked more beautiful and serene than I had ever seen her look before in my life.

I reached out my hand to her and we held hands as she smiled into my tear-filled eyes. I don't remember much about the ceremony except that the priest was very tall and very young.

After the ceremony was over we had to go "backstage" to sign the register. Then there was the usual photo session outside the church before the guests boarded the specially hired bus to take them to Dalkey.

Myself and Annette got into the white wedding car to cheers, jeers and sexual advice, from school children coming out of the school across the road. In the car I had a small case containing our passports, plane tickets and money and I put it behind us, between the back seat and the window, but forgot to take it with me when we got out of the car at the hotel in Dalkey. The reception went without a hitch and was enjoyed by all. Even the speeches went down well. However towards the end, when it came time for us to get dressed and leave for the airport, I discovered I did not have the case. At first I did not know where it could be. After a search of the hotel I realized I must have left it in the wedding car. We were able to phone the car company from the hotel and explain what we thought had happened. The car was searched and the case found. We arranged for them to leave it in the Gresham Hotel in O'Connell Street where we picked it up on our way to the airport later that evening.

We did not head straight to the airport from the Khyber Pass Hotel. We got a taxi to Bray first and had a light meal and a drink in the Bray Head Hotel. It was our first date as a married couple, a few yards from where we had met, just over three years before.

Our flight left Dublin airport about 10 -30 that night. All was well until we were about to land at Gerona airport in Northern Spain. There was thick fog covering the airport and as it did not have radar we could not land there. We had to fly on to Barcelona and when we eventually got off the plane in the early hours of the morning we were amazed by the sounds of the crickets and the heat. We then had to wait for our coach to come from Gerona to pick us up to take us to our hotel in Lloret de Mar. We spent the best part of our first night as man and wife sitting in Barcelona airport.

We did not get to the hotel until about 6 o'clock in the morning. By the time we reached it we were exhausted. We got into bed together for the first time and went to sleep.

When we woke up at about 10 o'clock the sun was streaming through the window and it felt incredibly hot. Although we were now married and there was no need for any more restraint we did not immediately make love. We did kiss and caress in the bed for a while and for the first time saw each other naked. Annette was beautiful. Her body was slim and so soft to the touch as I ran my hands over the perfect contours of her breast, buttocks and legs. We explored each other for some time, but did not go any further because we could hear the cleaners outside and we were afraid that someone might come in.

We showered and went down for a late breakfast and were amazed by the array of food available to us. After breakfast we familiarised ourselves with our surroundings. We explored the hotel and discovered the swimming pool which was on the roof, giving spectacular views of the sea and surrounding area. We were not on the sea front but we were only a short walk from it. We could see the sun-kissed water from the roof of the hotel. All this was so new to us, the luxury of the hotel, the spectacular scenery, the constant sunshine and the heat. We were like children let loose in a sweet shop. We wanted to sample everything.

First on the agenda was the roof-top pool. After we found it we went back to our room, put our bathing suits on and headed back to sunbathe and try out the pool. Despite all the sunshine the water in the pool was freezing and after a quick plunge we found a couple of sun beds close to the poolside bar. We got two Cuba Libres, tasted for the first time, and spent the rest of the morning drenching each other in sun tan lotion and basking in the warm sunshine.

After a few hours sunbathing and a few more Cuba Libres, we headed back to our room, slightly tipsy from the sun and the alcohol. By then it had been cleaned. The bed was made and the curtains had been closed over against the heat of the sun, so the room was not as warm as it had been earlier. The alcohol must have given me courage. As soon as we were in the room and the door was securely locked I held Annette in my arms and we fell onto the bed, locked in a passionate embrace. This time Annette did not put on the brakes and we attempted to make love for the first time. It was an attempt that did not succeed. As I tried to penetrate Annette, she said she was feeling pain so I stopped and we just lay together, holding each other on top of the bed. We continued kissing and touching each other but we did not try to have intercourse again and very soon fell asleep in each other's arms.

Later when we got up we laughed about our failed attempt and Annette said something about how she need not have been so concerned about us having sex before we were married as we probably would not have been able to do it anyway. This was our attitude to sex right from the start; we had a laugh and did not take it all that seriously, our love for each other was more important. That night, after dinner in the hotel we went down the town and Annette discovered a drink she became very fond of, a green-coloured mint liqueur served in a huge brandy-shaped glass, and over the course of the honeymoon she got through one or two of them.

The spectacle, colour and sounds of the town were all intoxicating to a young couple coming from the relative drabness of Dublin in the 1960s and we were in awe of it all. We stayed out late most nights, dancing in the clubs and bars where there was always music until the small hours of the morning. One club in particular, El Relicaro I think was its name, became a favourite of ours. At a certain time of the night, to the refrain of Al Martino singing *Blue Spanish Eyes* the roof slid open and a sky full of stars was revealed. To two unsophisticated young Dubliners this was amazing to behold.

The sea was also a huge attraction for us and we spent a lot of time on the warm sandy beach. Amazingly the sea water was actually warmer than the hotel pool. We really indulged ourselves on our honeymoon, rambling around the old town of Lloret, going on boat trips or lying on the beach by day. Then in the evening we enjoyed a pre-dinner drink at the pool bar on the roof and after dinner danced until late in the bars and clubs close to the sea. And all the time when we were alone together in our room in the early morning or late at night we were becoming familiar with each other's body, kissing, caressing, touching and exploring.

We never did have full intercourse on our honeymoon, but it did not bother us because we knew it would happen in its own good time. And all the bodily familiarity, although we did not know it then, was magnetising our bodies to each other and building the foundations for a life time of great love making which was to last right up to Annette's passing.

All too soon the honeymoon was over and it was time to go home, home being a bed-sit on Mountshannon Road, Rialto. We had rented it before we went on honeymoon because our house in Clinches Court was not ready to live in just yet due to the problems we'd had with the proposed redevelopment of the area and getting the guarantee from the council.

The week after we got home we attended the wedding of Dennis and Rosaleen, our first social event as husband and wife.

CHAPTER TEN

A cold, back bedroom and rat-infested kitchen in No. 40 Mountshannon Road became our home for the next four months. It also came with a peeping tom. We were spied on from a house behind our bedroom. We hated that bedsit. It was small, old-fashioned and cold and we spent as little time in it as we could. I was still working in the electrical goods company but Annette had had to give up her job in O'Dea's when she got married, "as them was the rules." After I went to work each morning Annette did not waste time in the bedsit, she either went into town or went to her mother's in Ballyfermot. Luckily this situation did not last too long as she managed to get a job as a cashier with RTV rentals in the State cinema building in Phibsboro. After a while she was moved to their office in O'Connell Street, beside the Savoy Cinema.

We really only slept in Mountshannon Road. Every night after work I would meet Annette in either my mother's or in her mother's in Ballyfermot where we would have a meal. We'd either stay there until it was bedtime or go to the pictures. Most weekends, after a lie-in on Saturday morning, we would go into town for lunch and on Saturday night we usually went dancing, mostly to the Crystal or the Metropole. After another late sleep-in on Sunday which usually included making love, we went to the Green Rooster Restaurant in O'Connell Street for lunch.

This was the pattern of our life for the duration of the time we were in the bedsit on Mountshannon Road. The peeping tom came to our attention a few days after we moved in. Being young and unconcerned about our surroundings, we left the light on when we were getting ready for bed. There was only net curtains on the window so everything and everyone was clearly visible from outside, a fact of which we were totally oblivious as we were still in honeymoon mode and were in the habit of kissing and cuddling as we prepared for bed.

One night as I was holding Annette close to me and kissing her neck and shoulders she thought she saw a curtain move in the house across the back garden. We stopped what we were doing and turned the light off, all the time looking across at the opposite window. Someone began to open it slightly and we could clearly see a man with a pair of binoculars looking at our bedroom. From then on we were more careful with our pre bed routine. We always made sure we put out the light before we began getting ready for bed, but sometimes, before the light went out, we would see movement in the curtains across the way and a man's head looking across in our direction.

By Christmas 1968, and after over three months of marriage, our families we felt were expecting "news" from us. Annette was getting comments about her weight. She had begun to put on a little, which because she had been so slim was noticeable. By this time we were having full intercourse, but we had nothing to report. All the problems relating to the house had also been resolved and we had decorated it and built a partition from the hall to close off the bedroom and were planning on moving in after Christmas

In contrast to our time in Mountshannon Road, from the start we loved living in Clinches Court. We had decorated it in a modern op art style. For wallpaper think of Del boy's flat in *Only Fools and Horses* and we'd lit the rooms with standard lamps, laid new carpet in the middle room and bedroom and painted the kitchen a bright yellow. We'd also hung new curtains on all the windows. The bedroom was warm and cosy and it had a fireplace which we used a lot that winter. Our new home also had the advantage of being near town and was very convenient for both our jobs.

In reality our marriage really only started when we moved to Clinches Court. We seldom ate in Mountshannon or entertained visitors or friends there so we never shopped for much food stuffs. In our new house we took great pleasure in doing a weekly shop in the supermarket and we also started inviting our family and friends down and cooking a meal for them. We were becoming a proper little 'Mr & Mrs'. We also had very nice neighbours. One in particular, Sally, a, to us, elderly lady who lived next door became very fond of Annette. She used to tell her all about the history of the houses and the area. She and her family had lived there since the houses were built and at that stage she was the last member of her family still living in the house where she was born.

Life was good for us in so many ways in Clinches Court. We were very much in love and enjoying a great love life, we were both working at jobs we liked, we had our own home, we were not short of money and our families were close enough to visit and be visited by us, as often as we liked. Our marriage was off to a great start, and we were ready and anxious to start a family.

While we were waiting, we decided we would go on a holiday. As Neil Armstrong was making plans to land on the Moon, we were on a horse-drawn caravanning holiday in Donegal, with both our mothers in tow. Whose idea it was I don't know but we asked our two mothers, our two mothers- in -law! to come on holiday with us, on our first holiday together since our honeymoon, and in a horse-drawn caravan with barely enough room for two. We were so innocent back then. It had all the makings of a major disaster written all over it, but it wasn't. We had a great time, and our two mothers got on like a house on fire, ever after they were the best of friends.

We booked the caravan for two weeks in July and the plan was that the two mothers would be with us for the first week. Then we would put them on a bus home and we would have the second week for ourselves. All was well as we set out from Busaras, on a sunny Saturday morning, heading for Bunbeg to pick up our horse and wagon. The bus trip to Donegal was long but uneventful and we reached our destination on Saturday evening. We went to the caravan park to pick up our mobile accommodation and were met by the owner who introduced us to "Pettle" our horse.

As it was late we decided we would not begin our travels until the next morning, so Pettle was left in the field and we took possession of the wagon. I don't know what we'd been expecting, but when we saw the amount of space for four people in the caravan we started to think that maybe this was not such a good idea after all. It looked so cramped. There was what looked like a child's play cabinet with cups and saucers and such like, a tiny sink unit and beside it, two gas rings on a piece of wood. Running along one side of the caravan was a very narrow bunk bed and there were two pieces of chain attached to a panel which pulled down to give another bunk which was stored overhead. There was also a curtained off area to the front. We pulled back the curtains and revealed "the master bedroom" – a very small wooden plinth, with a mattress and pillows.

We piled our luggage as best we could against the side of the caravan. A few humorous comments were passed about who was sleeping where but we knew we had no choice but to make the best of what we had. The mothers were great and never complained. They threw themselves wholeheartedly into the spirit of the holiday. Annette's mother decided she would sleep on top and once the sleeping arrangements were sorted we, with great care and lots of "don't be looking I'm changing my top" moments, washed and cleaned ourselves as best we could. Then the four of us went out to a local bar and restaurant for the first meal and drinks of our holiday. Needless to say we were a bit "merry" coming back from the pub and were not too concerned about who saw what as we "hooshed" Mary into her top bunk. My mother collapsed sleepily into hers. Annette and I then crawled into the 'master bedroom', wrapped ourselves around each other and went asleep.

After breakfast the next morning the owner came around with Pettle and showed us how to dress the horse in her harness. I watched carefully so when he asked me if I was happy that I could harness the horse, I of course said yes no problem, it did not look too difficult. We were ready to go. Myself and Annette were decked out in new t- shirts and shorts and the ladies were in summer dresses as we set off on our merry way to explore the hills of Donegal in our 'Wanderly Wagon'.

The first problem then presented itself. There was only room for three on the seat of the caravan. This meant that I would have to walk and lead Pettle along. I did not know it then but even if there had been room for four on the seat this is the way I would have ended up spending my holiday, either pulling Pettle up a hill or trying to stop her galloping down one. We learned pretty quickly that hilly Donegal is not the best place for a horse-drawn caravan holiday.

We did not cover a great distance that first day as we were no sooner on our way than we came to a church where Mass was soon to start, and, it being Sunday, Annette wanted to go. So we stopped and I read the paper and minded the horse and caravan while the women went to pray.

After Mass we set off again and about a mile or so later we came to a bar with outside seating. Someone wanted to go to the toilet so we stopped at the bar. The sun was shining and it was warm so someone suggested that a cold drink would go down well.

Another stop.

After a while we set off again and covered a few more miles. I was sweating and sunburned, trying to control Pettle, while the ladies, with Annette holding the reins, sat taking in the scenery and talking. At about six o'clock we came to another bar with a field at the side in which there was another horse-drawn caravan. Seeing this we decided we had travelled enough for one day and we would stay here for the night.

The women got down from their seat to stretch their legs and Annette held Pettle steady while I went into the bar to enquire about getting permission to put the horse into the field for the night. I also wanted to see who was in the other caravan which was parked there. The barman said there was no problem about putting Pettle into the field and pointed out a couple in their forties, who were sitting at a table drinking, as the occupants of the other caravan.

I went out and told the rest of them it was ok to stay here for the night so we unharnessed Pettle brought her to the field and fed her with some of the feed the owner had given us. I also got her some water from the bar. When all this was done we cleaned ourselves and went inside. I pointed out the other couple to Annette as the occupants of the other caravan. Annette suggested we should talk to them as they might be able to give us a few tips. Annette and I went over and introduced ourselves as the new caravan arrivals and asked them how they were finding the holiday so far. They told us they had been at this bar for the past three days. They had put their horse into the field when they arrived and when they went to get him the next morning he was gone. They had not been able to find him since and were afraid to let the owner know they had lost his horse. They intended to leave the next day and phone the owner to let him know where his caravan was.

We stayed there for the night and made sure Pettle was secure in the field before we went to bed. First thing next morning I got up and checked that she was still there, she was.

After breakfast, ours and Pettle's, we got ready to go so I proceeded to put the harness on Pettle. When I was 'finished' I had a few bits of harness in my hands that I did not know what to do with. The horse seemed to be "fully-clothed" but I still had bits of harness left over. We continued on our way despite this as Pettle seemed to have no difficulty pulling the wagon and everything looked secure.

Again we did not cover a great distance as the terrain was very hilly. I also had great difficulty controlling Pettle, especially going downhill when she wanted to gallop. Even with Annette's help, as she held tight on the reins I struggled to hold her back. For safety sake when we were going downhill, the two mothers usually walked. They had a great time laughing and chatting as Annette and I struggled with Pettle.

On one of the days when the weather was really sunny and warm we were looking for a beach we had been told about in Kinkasslagh. We asked directions to the beach and were told to take the next turn right. We eventually came to the next right turn which was a narrow road up a rather steep hill. We turned and proceeded up it, Annette and the two mothers walking and me pulling Pettle. As we neared the top we were approached by a farmer and told we were on private property and would have to go back. We explained we were looking for a beach and he told us it was further down, we had taken a wrong turn. It was impossible to turn where we were so we had to go to the top of the hill to turn which we did. We sent the two Marys back to the bottom of the hill to wait while we turned and got ready to make our way back down. I told Annette to sit on the seat and hold the reins as tight as she could while I stood in front of Pettle, holding the bit in her mouth in an effort to take us down the hill as slowly as possible. Pettle was having none of it. About a third of the way down with Annette holding the reins for dear life and me doing all I could to contain the horse, Pettle took off. She left me with no option but to, John Wayne like, jump off the ground and put my feet on each side of the shafts, while looking into the horse's mouth. Annette stood up, holding the reins and screamed as the caravan sped down the hill. It was out of our control and racing towards the two mothers who were standing at the side of the road also screaming at what was unfolding before their eyes.

As we reached the bottom of the hill, and were about to go careering back onto the main road, the caravan came to a sudden stop. A stump of a tree which was protruding from the ground had embedded itself in the side of the caravan, bringing it to a halt. We were all badly shaken but unhurt, and after managing to get the caravan, now with a large gash in the side, away from the tree stump we proceeded to the beach. With the help of strong tea, we let our nerves calm a bit, as the mothers gave thanks for the aversion of what could have been a disaster.

On the last night of our mothers' stay we were in Crolly. We were parked beside the pub owned by Leo Brennan, the father of the Brennan family who later became the famous group Clannad. We had the privilege of being amongst the first people from outside Donegal to witness the emerging talent of one of Ireland's best group of musicians.

But the really memorable thing about our night in Brennan's pub was a fight that broke out later that night. We and a pub full of other people were enjoying the music when, and I mean this quite literally, the place exploded in violence. The most violent pub fight I ever witnessed took place all around us, in Irish. Tables were thrown, chairs were broken over people's heads, glasses were flying over our heads and faces were being punched, by men and women. We saw one person being held by the scruff of the neck and the arse of his trousers and thrown through a glass door. It was like a scene from a John Ford western. When I realised what was happening I grabbed the women and pushed them into a toilet we were lucky enough to be sitting beside.

The fight ended as suddenly as it began and the pub quickly emptied as everyone made their way home. Later that night, when it was almost dark and we were sitting outside the caravan having a cup of tea, a lone garda on a bike with no light came cycling into the village to investigate the incident. Despite asking, we never did get to know what had caused the mayhem, what happens in Crolly stays in Crolly.

It was an eventful but very enjoyable first week of our holiday. As we prepared to send our mothers home, we were looking forward to a more relaxing and violence-free week alone.

After goodbyes the following morning, our mothers got the bus to Letterkenny, to connect with the bus to Dublin. We said goodbye to Crolly and headed off in our caravan, relieved that the week with our mothers was over but glad we had done it. Now that there was only the two of us the caravan did not seem so small and stripping and dressing was a lot easier as we did not have to be careful about who might see what.

On Tuesday of the second week we came to Dungloe where the "Mary from Dungloe" festival was in full swing. We parked our caravan in the field beside the marquee and set Pettle free in the adjacent field, safe in the knowledge that it was enclosed with fencing and she would not be able to wander too far. We were no sooner settled in the field when an opportunity to make money presented itself, if we had been brave enough to take a chance. People came knocking on the door enquiring if we were telling fortunes. We could have made a fortune if we had had hard necks. We could have taken their money and spoofed a little, just like real fortune-tellers but we didn't.

We went to the dance in the marquee that night and had a great laugh at the state of some of the old country men. They were prowling around the marquee, some of them barely able to walk, eyeing up and trying to chat up the young girls. It was something we remarked on about that dance, most of the men seemed to be old and most of the girls were young.

The next morning we intended to move on but when I went to get Pettle I discovered she was lame. I looked at her leg and noticed her hoof was cut. She had caught it in the barbed wire which was around some of the fencing in the field. We were now well into our second week, and quite honestly I was getting tired of walking Pettle around Donegal every day. Also the caravan was the worst for wear, as apart from the gash in the side, we'd had another incident. We had gone into someone's garden so we could turn and ended up stuck under a low branch of a tree which damaged the roof. Now Pettle was injured. We decided to end our life as nomads.

We called the owner and told him about Pettle so her cut could be treated. We asked him to take us to a nice beach in the caravan and leave us there to enjoy the rest of our holiday. He agreed to do that.

He arrived the next day and took Pettle, who was not badly hurt, just a slight cut in her hoof. Then he hitched our caravan to his jeep and said he would find a nice spot for us to spend the rest of our holiday. Annette wanted to stay in the caravan, to clean up and wash the breakfast delph while we were moving. But luckily the owner said it might get very bumpy in the caravan and it would be better if she did not stay in it.

How right he was. As we were driving along we came to a sharp bend in the road which was bordered on one side by a drop of about eight feet. All of a sudden the caravan flashed past the jeep and crashed over the side of the road. It smashed down on its side, over the eight foot drop. It was in bits. If Annette had been in it I have no doubt she would have been killed or at the very least seriously hurt.

Although we were on a country road with very few houses around, in a matter of minutes the place was full of people inspecting our wrecked caravan. So there we were having started out the week before with a horse and caravan and now we had lost the horse through lameness and the caravan was a write off. A beach holiday was also now out of the question.

After we retrieved our clothes and what food we could salvage from the wreckage of the caravan, we were taken back to the caravan base. We were allowed to use one of the caravans there for the next few days. Most of our food had been destroyed in the caravan crash so we had to replenish our stock and by this time our cash was running out. For some unknown reason we had not bought return bus tickets so we had to keep enough money to get home. But true to form we didn't. Instead we spent all we had and decided to hitch home. This turned out to be a source of some embarrassment.

On the morning of our departure the owner of the caravan, thinking we were catching the bus to Dublin, because we'd told him so, offered to give us a lift to the bus station. He went flat out to make sure we got to the bus, dropping us right beside it, only a minute or two before departure. We got out of the car, thanking him for his trouble, and stood beside the bus waving him off as if he was our dearest friend and we didn't want to lose sight of him until he faded into the distance. Once he was gone we waved the bus on, much to the annoyance of the driver who had been waiting for us to board it. Carrying our cases, we then made our way out of Bunbeg to the Dublin road for the long hitch home.

A milk lorry driver took pity on us a while later and gave us a lift to just outside Aughnacloy. We waited for what seemed like hours with only enough money for a bar of chocolate and a cup of coffee. Eventually we got a lift and the driver turned out to be someone quite famous at the time, Michael Dillon. He was the presenter of a farming programme on Telefís Eireann. He picked us up in Aughnacloy and gave us a lift all the way to Glasnevin in Dublin.

We thanked him profusely as we got out of his car and promised we would become avid viewers of his programme from then on. With the few coppers we had left we were able to get a bus into town and we arrived home, tired and starving.

When we entered no. 7 Clinches Court we were delighted to see a bottle of milk, a loaf of bread, butter, rashers, sausages and eggs, on the kitchen table. My mother had left them for us, letting herself in with a spare key my father had used while we were decorating. Bliss!

Many years later when our youngest son Robert, commenced school in Tallaght he came across some photographs which we had taken on that holiday. He got great amusement telling his classmates that his parents used to be Travellers, though that's not the word he used. And he had the pictures to prove it.

CHAPTER ELEVEN

After our holiday we fell back into our routine of work, visiting our families and being visited by them. Things were quite normal for a while. Then, before Christmas, Annette became pregnant. We were overjoyed and wasted no time in telling our families the great news. After visits to the doctor we learned we would be parents by early June 1970.

We could not wait and neither could our families, as this would be the first baby on either side. A great sense of excitement developed, especially with Annette's younger sisters.

Shortly after the announcement presents started arriving for our new baby, gender as yet unknown. My Aunt Ann was a fabulous knitter and as soon as she heard Annette was pregnant she began knitting clothes in all colours for the new arrival. When David was born, we had "tons" of clothes to dress him up in.

Unfortunately Annette's pregnancy was marred by sadness. Shortly after enjoying a great and very happy Christmas, with lots of talk and plans for the new arrival in the summer, Annette's father, Bill, became ill. At first it was not considered anything serious, just a bad cold like many more that very cold winter, but then pneumonia set in. A few days later, on the 6th January, 1970, I had the most unpleasant task of telling Annette her father was dead.

Suddenly, in the midst of what had been a period of great joy and happiness, we were confronted with the most unexpected loss and grief. We were all devastated by how suddenly and unexpectedly death had arrived. It was in stark contrast to the long wait of nine months for the joy of new life.

Over the mourning period and the funeral I was very worried about Annette. She was very close to her father, as he had been to her, and I did not know how this was going to impact on her pregnancy. I need not have worried. After the initial shock Annette was a tower of strength for her mother and her younger sisters. While extremely sad that her father would never see his first grandchild she held up and controlled her grief in a heroic way. It was a hallmark of the courage she would display in times of trouble and stress over the rest of her life. After Bill's funeral the sheen seemed to go off the pregnancy for a while and we spent a lot of time with Mary and the younger sisters, Louise, Caroline and Claire.

A week or so after the funeral Annette went back to work. She was working in the RTV rental office in O'Connell Street and I was still with the electrical goods company, Neasden Distributors. After our wedding they had moved from Essex Street to James Street. Possibly as a consequence of her father's death, combined with her own condition, Annette began to get sick and miss work. I was concerned for Annette and the soon-to-be born baby, so on a number of occasions I missed work as well so I could be with her. Annette intended to leave work after the baby was born so her absence was not too serious, but I, now more than ever, needed a job. When my boss in Neasden, Flor O'Mahony, a really nice Cork man, who was very patient with me over the lost time, put it to me that I would have to choose between my job and my wife, there was only one decision to make.

I very soon found a job, just across the road from Clinches Court, in Trux Warehouse on the North Strand. I gave my notice in after six very happy years with Neasden and began working as a Warehouse Manager. It was a job I hated, but it allowed me to be near Annette during the latter part of her pregnancy. Annette's impending childbirth I think, in some little way, lessened the sadness felt by the death of Bill. It gave Mary something else to think about. As Annette's due date neared Mary spent a lot of time with her as indeed did my own mother.

We'd been told the baby was due in early June but Annette's concept of time took over at this point. Early June came and went with no sign of the new, and eagerly awaited, arrival. Annette's health had improved considerably and she was now blooming. She was looking great and had no pre-birth nerves at all while I was a nervous wreck. I was worrying how we would get to the Rotunda Hospital should Annette decide to have the baby during the night. Although the Rotunda was not far away, we did not have a car or a phone. But there was still no sign of Annette looking like she was going to give birth any time soon She was not in the least perturbed. Her philosophy was: "when the apple is ripe it will fall."

She had of course left work at this time and spent her days at home, relaxing and waiting for the big day to come. I was working just across the road and was able to nip across for my breaks and at lunch hour, so that Annette was never too long on her own. My mother also dropped down from time to time to make sure everything was alright.

On Thursday night, the 18th of June I came home from work and we had our tea. After our meal we went across the road to the Fairview Strand cinema to see a film, returning home at about 10.30 p.m. Shortly after we got home, as we prepared to go to bed, Annette began to get contractions. I wanted to get a taxi immediately and head for the Rotunda but Annette felt it was better to wait and see would the contractions continue.

After a while, and a few more contractions, with a minor panic building up in me, Annette decided she wanted to walk down to Dominick Street. If the contractions got more regular she would be near the Rotunda. Just before eleven o'clock, I picked up Annette's hospital bag and we set out on a leisurely walk from the North Strand to Dominick Street, arriving at about 11.40 p.m. My mother was still up and immediately sized up the situation. She made Annette comfortable on the couch and got us some tea.

By this time the contractions were becoming more regular, with shorter intervals. At about 12.30 a.m. the three of us went across the road and Annette presented herself to the night porter at the Rotunda Hospital.

After a short wait a nurse appeared, took Annette's case from me and led her down the corridor, with me and my mother following behind. We reached an old-fashioned lift, with a pull across gate which the nurse opened. She turned to me and said:

"you can say goodbye to your wife now." I held Annette and gave her a kiss on the lips. The nurse then led her into the lift, pulled across the gate, and as my mother and I stood watching helplessly Annette disappeared from view.

We had no option but to head back to the flat in Dominick Street. That's the way things were done back then, no way was a husband allowed to be with his wife when she gave birth. I stayed in Dominick Street that night, sleeping in my old bed.

First thing the next morning I got up and went across to the Rotunda, but Annette had not given birth yet so I went on to work in Trux Warehouse. During the course of the morning I made a few phone calls to the Rotunda but there was still no news.

I finished work early that day and went back to the hospital, picking up a large bunch of flowers on the way. At reception I learned that Annette had still not given birth but I was allowed to go to the ward and see her for a few minutes. As I walked down a corridor, heading for the labour ward, with the bunch of flowers in my hand, unknown to me and approaching from another corridor leading to the same labour ward was another young man, also with a bunch of flowers. We both reached the ward at the exact same time and just as a nurse was coming out. Both of us could see the nurse but we could not see each other. At the same moment we asked the nurse the same question: "could I see Mrs Halpin please?" I turned around to see who this other man, with a bunch of flowers in his hand was, asking to see my wife, just as he looked at me, obviously feeling the same. We were strangers to each other and stared at each other quizzically. The nurse stood and looked at us both with an equally puzzled look on her face. After a moment or two the problem was solved; there were two Mrs. Halpins in the labour ward waiting to give birth.

I was allowed in for just a few moments, barely enough time to hold Annette's hand and give her a kiss. It was enough time to tell her how much I loved her and how I was looking forward to having her and the baby home again. I was then whisked out of the ward.

When I made enquiries again later in the afternoon Annette had given birth to our first child, a boy whom we called David William Halpin. David was after no one in particular, we just liked the name and William after Annette's father, William "Bill" Kennedy.

As soon as I was allowed, I went up to see Annette and our new son. Annette looked marvellous. The birth, although it had taken a long time did not seem to have taken too much out of her and she, like me was on a high over our new baby. The first time I saw David I thought he was the image of my father. I was in no doubt he was our son. After the two Mrs. Halpins incident I was a little worried that the two Halpin babies might get mixed up but the resemblance to my father was uncanny.

After seeing Annette and letting my mother know the good news I then had to let Annette's family know. As we had no phones, that meant a trip to Ballyfermot. But as I was on my way over O'Connell Bridge to get the bus I met Mary and Claire on their way to visit the hospital. I was able to tell them the great news and to the amusement of everyone on the bridge the news was greeted by cheers and a dance of joy with hugs and kisses all-round.

CHAPTER TWELVE

A nnette recovered from the birth remarkably quickly. After a day or two she was looking so good that an older and wiser woman in the ward told her that if she continued to look like that she was in danger of being back again the same time next year. She wasn't too far wrong.

After about five days Annette was allowed home. Back then it was the custom to have babies christened very soon after the birth, so on the way to Ballyfermot where we were to stay with Annette's mother for a short time until Annette was used to handling the baby, we dropped into the church we'd been married in two years previously and had David christened. The Christening was a bit of an ordeal. My Aunt Ann, who had knitted all the clothes for David, was home from England where she was then living, with a friend of hers. Ann and her friend Gladys had come down to the hospital on the morning Annette was released and asked if they could come to the Christening. We felt obliged to say yes, so we all bundled into the taxi and headed for Ballyfermot. Ann had asked to hold David when we were in the taxi and Annette had passed her the baby. But when we got to the church Ann was reluctant to give David to Annette's sister Marie, who was to be the godmother. I can remember Marie coming to Annette and me saying in a distressed voice: "she won't give me the baby." We managed to get that situation resolved and Marie got to be David's godmother.

After the Christening we went back to Annette's house and later in the afternoon my parents and my brother came out to help us celebrate. After the festive tea I made a major blunder and in the process inadvertently hurt Annette. It was decided by someone, and I don't know who, that the celebrations should continue in Young's pub down the road. So we all, except for the younger sisters and Annette, who could not go because she was breast-feeding David, headed down to the pub. I, to my shame and embarrassment and without a thought for Annette, joined the posse and proceeded to be the proud and merry new father.

After a couple of hours drinking most of us headed back to the house. My parents, Ann and her friend got the bus back to town. When we arrived home Annette was up in bed. I went up to find her crying and distressed. Being the fool I was I could not understand what was wrong. I thought she should have been as happy as I was. Through her tears, she told me that she'd wanted me to stay with her on our first night home with our new baby. She was disappointed that I went to the pub leaving her all alone. Only then did I realise my mistake and although I had a few pints in me, I immediately felt stone cold sober. I was embarrassed and ashamed at what I had done, but most of all I felt so sorry for hurting Annette in this way. The sight of her crying at a time when she should be so happy was a cause of hurt to me, particularly as I had caused the pain. I think this was the first of the many times I inadvertently hurt Annette throughout our marriage. Each time I did so the sight of her crying tore at my heart's strings as I truly loved her and would never purposely hurt her. But from time to time, through thoughtlessness and lack of awareness, I did so, and each time swore I would never do so again. This time, like many more times in the years to come, Annette forgave me for my lack of thought, and things returned to normal.

A few days later we went home to the North Strand with our new baby. Annette was now a confident and protective mother. I returned to work in Trux, and I came home at lunch time each day to Annette and David. I did not want to return when the hour was up. We doted on our first child, as did both our families. No child ever got as much love and attention as David William Halpin did that first year of his life. We brought him everywhere, showing him off to all our friends and relatives as if he was the first baby ever born. We must have been insufferable bores, but we did not care. Sometimes when a child is born, particularly a first child, the mother transfers all her love and attention to the new love of her life, and the father is sidelined. This I am happy to say did not happen in our case, if anything the birth of David brought us closer together. Annette involved me in all aspects of David's development, including changing his nappy from day one. Naturally the extra work involved in taking care of David, including breast-feeding seemingly every hour, was exhausting on Annette. Consequently for a while we did not, make love as often as before, but as Autumn came and gave way to Winter, and the nights got chilly we would often light the fire in the bedroom and with David fed and snugly contented in his Moses basket, vow undying love to each other as we engaged in long, passionate, love making sessions while the coal fire cast shadows on the bedroom walls and ceiling

In the spring Annette became pregnant again and I left Trux. I started to work for International Meat Producers, Grand Canal Street, where I remained until they closed eleven years later. Although David was not yet a year old, we were delighted that we were going to have another baby as we'd never intended to have only one child. Gina was a Christmas baby, born on the 20th of December 1971. Like David, Gina was born in the Rotunda but unlike David's birth we did not have the time to take a leisurely walk to my mother's for tea before the birth.

We had a visit from Annette's mother and her sisters, Louise and Claire, on Sunday 19th December. After they left, with her mother believing Annette was going to be waiting until after Christmas, her waters broke. It was at about 9.30 that night. We still had no car or phone but we were on good terms with our neighbours to our left, the Curleys. They were a couple in their thirties, with two young children, and a car. They'd said to us not to hesitate to knock if we had to go to the hospital and Johnny would drive us there. When Annette's waters broke I immediately ran next door for help and I was very glad to notice Johnny's car was parked outside. His wife, Dolores, opened the door and I blurted out what had happened and asked if Johnny was available to take us to the Rotunda. Johnny, hearing me at the door then appeared, with a cigarette in his mouth and very obviously having had the benefit of a few pints. No problem says Johnny, get Annette and we'll go straight away.

When I saw Johnny my heart missed a beat, I knew we had to get to the hospital straight away, but not in his car. David was fast asleep in his cot and that's where we intended to leave him if Dolores would keep an eye on him. So I changed tack and said we would get a taxi if she would mind David. But Johnny insisted he could drive and while Dolores went to see how Annette was, turned his car in the direction of the North Strand Road. Dolores then emerged with Annette and assured us that Johnny had driven with much more drink than he had on him tonight and everything was alright!.

Annette and I looked at each other as Dolores continued to assure us everything would be alright and David would be well looked after. As it was a Sunday night there would not be too much traffic on the roads and the Rotunda was only a short drive so we took our lives and our as yet unborn baby's life and put them in the hands of Johnny Curley and got into the car. In five minutes flat we were at the Rotunda, safe and sound. I thanked Johnny and helped Annette into the now familiar reception area. We waited for the nurse to come down and take Annette up in the old-fashioned lift, with the cage-like door.

After kissing Annette goodbye I went across to Dominick Street to let my mother and father know the news. I did not delay long as I was anxious to get back to David. When I did get back to him, about half an hour later, he was still fast asleep oblivious of the fact that his space was soon to be invaded by a baby sister.

In those days, without mobile phones or indeed phones of any kind, you had to go directly to the hospital for news, and that's what I did. Early the following morning I dressed and fed David, put him into his pram and went down to the hospital, where I learned from the receptionist that I was the father of a baby girl. Gina's was a quicker birth than David, and in the early hours of Monday, December 20th, Regina Maria Halpin made her appearance onto the world stage. We were delighted with our new baby girl, and people told us our family was complete.

I went straight over to my mother and told her the good news. She already knew as she had been over to the hospital before me. I left David with my parents and went straight back to the Rotunda where I was allowed to see Annette and the baby for a short time. Even though it was so soon after giving birth, I remember thinking how great Annette looked. She was feeding Gina without any bother and was completely relaxed. She had wanted to feed all our children, but when she started with David she'd found it difficult at first. She'd persisted and succeeded and now she looked expert at the task. Annette was delighted to see me and told me later that she could not wait to tell me we had a new baby daughter.

Later that day I went and told Annette's family the good news. During Annette's stay in hospital my mother helped me with David and I visited Annette every day, collecting David in the evening and returning to the North Strand. After David was asleep, I cleaned and decorated the house in the hope and anticipation that Annette would be home for Christmas. We had to plead with the doctors to let Annette out on Christmas Eve. If she did not get out then she would be in the hospital all over Christmas. It was only at the last minute that Annette was released and after equipping the new baby with presents for her big brother, a banana and a car, I collected Annette by taxi.

We went home on the afternoon of Christmas Eve to a house over-decorated with trees, lights, tinsel and a plastic crib. This time we did not stop at a church for a Christening but made plans to have a family get-together and Christening early in the New Year.

It was the first year that we stayed in our own house on Christmas Day, and, as Annette had been in hospital and I had no time to shop and cook, my mother had cooked a piece of ham and a small turkey for us. I was to collect them on Christmas Eve night, after we'd got settled in with the children and put them to bed. Every thing was going great: Annette was overjoyed with the house and the decorations, the two babies could not have been better and they went down without a bother. I then went to Dominick Street to collect the meat for Christmas Day.

Everyone was in great mood when I got there, all delighted that everything had gone so well with the birth and that Annette had got out for Christmas. The mood was intoxicating and very soon I'd agreed to go over to the Seven Stars Bar with my father and brother for one drink. That one drink turned out to be more like four or five, with the result that I was not home until after midnight. Some people never learn from their mistakes. Again I had let Annette down at a very vulnerable time for her. Once more Annette found the grace to forgive me with dignity. But I was running out of rope.

Christmas Day as I remember it went exceptionally well. In the afternoon our neighbours, Sally, Johnny and Dolores, dropped in to see the new arrival and brought presents. We just relaxed in front of the TV with a glass or two of wine, looking in every now and then on David in his cot and Gina in her Moses' basket, just recently vacated by David. We went to bed early, both of us exhausted as Annette was still recuperating after the birth. We did not go visiting on Stephen's Day, but Annette's mother came down to us for a while. She was delighted with her new granddaughter.

I had had a few days off from work for Christmas but soon it was time to return and leave Annette alone with the two babies. My new job was further away from home so it was not possible for me to come home at lunch hour as I had done when I was with Trux just across the road. Without knowing it at the time, this situation proved to be a turning point in the relationship between Annette and my mother.

I related earlier the somewhat shaky start to the relationship between my mother and Annette. It had improved considerably since then, but now that relationship really blossomed. Annette said to me years later, after my mother had died, that over the years she'd felt more like a daughter than a daughter-in-law. I believe it was during this time that those feelings began to develop.

Annette's mother had gone back to work in O'Dea's since Bill's death, as she still had a young family to support. This meant she was not free to help Annette with the babies as much as she would have liked to. But my mother was free as she did not work outside the home. She was able to help whenever Annette wanted her to. After an initial hesitancy to ask, Annette got more comfortable with my mother, with the result, my mother used come down to the North Strand two or three times a week to help Annette and give her a break from the children. When we wanted to go out in the evening, which was not very often, my mother would also baby-sit for us. And all the while during this time Annette and my mother were bonding like mother and daughter.

Annette had her hands full and as we had two babies under two, we had to be careful she did not become pregnant quite so soon again, so when our love life resumed, we decided we would practice birth control, but with Annette's moral values, the pill or condoms were excluded. We had to read up on "the safe period" and other methods approved by his Holiness. After trying to cope with these "approved" ways of making love for a while we were both frustrated. We gradually went back to being spontaneous, and we got away with it for a while. But then, in early 1973, Annette learned she was pregnant again. Despite the fact it would mean three babies under four we were delighted.

The one problem a new baby presented was space. We only had one bedroom in the North Strand and it was already a little crowded with the double-bed and the cot, which David and Gina were still small enough to sleep in together. We knew we now had a decision to make. We could open the attic space in the roof or we could move. We loved living in the North Strand and were reluctant to move at first, but after talking it over and taking everything into consideration, including the lack of a safe play area when the children got a bit older as we were in a narrow lane with an increasing amount of traffic coming through it, we very reluctantly decided to look for a new house.

When we eventually told our neighbours we were going to move because Annette was pregnant again, Sally was very sorry to hear it. She regaled us with stories about how her mother and father had brought up ten children in her house, which was the same size as ours and she could see no reason why we could not raise three in the same space. When we told our families that Annette was pregnant again, and we'd waited a while to do so, the reaction, especially from my mother, while not disapproval was laced with a concern that I should have given Annette a bit more time before making her pregnant again.

We started looking at the adverts in the papers for new houses in the many estates beginning to mushroom all around the city. We spent many a weekend taking bus trips to the various building sites to view a wide range of houses, at a wide range of prices, most of them out of our reach. Not only had we to buy a new house, but we had to sell No. 7 Clinches Court as well. After the trouble we had in buying it we knew that would not be easy.

But a solution was at hand. Annette's brother Liam had worked in the print shop at Guinness brewery from 1965 until the end of 1971 when he took advantage of a redundancy offer to pursue his first love, music, and to travel. Towards the end of 1972, having spent some time in Greece, Liam returned home and resumed his relationship with his girlfriend, Mary Wall. Mary and Liam married in April 1973. Knowing we wanted to sell Clinches Court and as they were now married and renting a house, Liam and Mary offered to buy it. One reason being, Mary was from Clontarf and she wanted to stay near her family.

Their offer presented us with a dilemma. At the time Liam approached us about buying the house we had seen a house in Tallaght we wanted to buy, but we needed a deposit of £1500 which we did not have. We had put our house up for sale, with an asking price of enough to pay off the mortgage and have £1500 to cover the deposit but so far we had no takers.

As Annette's pregnancy progressed and with no sign of a buyer, it looked like we would be staying in Clinches Court. Liam and Mary continued to ask about buying it. But while we had no difficulty in asking the high price for the house on the open market we felt that if we were selling to family we should lower it, which if we wanted to buy in Tallaght we could not do. There would also be a problem with Liam and Mary getting a loan as Liam was not working in a normal job though he was making some money as a musician. How it came about I do not know, but as they wanted us to sell to them and we all knew the loan would be a problem, a somewhat unorthodox solution was reached – Liam and Mary would give us £1500 pounds, we would pay the deposit on the house in Tallaght and when we moved out of Clinches Court they would move in and continue to pay the mortgage. Unorthodox in the extreme and only workable if we trusted each other implicitly. We drew up an agreement between us which years later was "legalised" by a solicitor. When he was drafting the "proper" document he remarked that he had never come across anything like our little arrangement before. It worked for us and when Liam and Mary moved in they opened up the attic making a large new bedroom with a New York style studio apartment look about it. I would now venture to suggest Clinches Court is worth more than our house in Tallaght.

Our time in Clinches Court had been very happy and we left with many happy memories of the start of our marriage and young family. We hoped that this would continue in our new home.

When all the details had been worked out between us, we made plans to move to Tallaght before the baby was born. So on the evening of 3rd of September, 1973, with the aid of an open lorry hired through an ad in the *Evening Herald,* we loaded our belongings and headed out to Tallaght, to begin our life in the suburbs.

After unloading the lorry we began to put the few bits and pieces into the various rooms of what to us seemed a huge house. As darkness began to fall, I switched on the light only to discover that there was not a light bulb in the house. We were left with no option but to put the mattress on the floor of the front room and go to bed, which was not an easy task for Annette now eight months pregnant. The following morning after breakfast I went down to Tallaght Village to the only shop there then, H. Williams, for a supply of bulbs.

Life was different in Tallaght, different and lonely, but at least David and Gina had somewhere to play. At that stage David was gone three and Gina was almost two. Both of them took delight in living on a building site which Raheen Green then was. Right outside our front door was an area known as the muck hills, now the green. But back then it was where the builders kept all their machinery and building materials. It was a paradise for young children who liked to play with muck and dirty water. I was still working in Grand Canal Street so I had to be up very early each morning to get one of the few 65 buses that were servicing the route, leaving Annette and the children in the wilderness that was Tallaght in those early years.

CHAPTER THIRTEEN

lthough deceased almost three months now, Annette is
credited with co-authorship of however this book turns
out because I told her what I was trying to do and asked
for her help. Annette has had great influence on events since her
passing, but now I want to record the fact that as I began to try
to write this section on our first years in Tallaght I was having
great difficulty in getting a start, in getting a handle on how to
start. I reminded Annette that she was co-author and asked her
to help me, to be with me and to refresh my memory about the
time we moved to Tallaght.

On the 7th of July, 2009, a friend of Annette's, Ann Garvey,
who to the best of my recollection never visited before phoned
me at about 1.30 p.m. as I was struggling with this section.
She asked if she could come and visit with me as she had
been away when Annette passed away. She arrived at three
o'clock and during the course of our conversation mentioned
an essay Annette had written many years before, in 1991 to
be exact. It had been re-published in a book, *Since Adam
was a boy* to celebrate the 30th anniversary of Tallaght
Welfare Society in 1999. Ann, who works as a community
development worker, said that she used that essay in her
classes all the time, to illustrate to her students what life was
like in Tallaght in the beginning, before all the amenities we
now have existed. When Ann mentioned this I immediately
remembered the essay. She asked if I had a copy of the book
and after a short search I found it where it had lain unopened
and indeed forgotten by me. In the essay Annette records the
early years of our time in Tallaght. It was just what I wanted
and needed at that very time. I believe Annette guided me
to it through her friend, sending Ann to tell me that what I
was looking for was on the cluttered book shelves, justifying
her credit as co-author of this memoir. To quote a statement
Annette wrote in that essay: 'There are certain things in life

we can never fully understand until we have experienced them ourselves.'

I have experienced Annette's help and guidance more than once since starting to write this memoir. As I have said to Annette often since her passing, it will take more than death to keep us apart and it's death that will bring us together again. I will now let Annette tell you what it was like for her when we first moved out to Tallaght:

'We moved to Tallaght in the Autumn of 1973, a month before my third baby was born. There are certain things in life we can never fully understand until we experience them ourselves. Moving out to Tallaght was one of these things for me. I could never have imagined what it was like to feel so isolated, abandoned and lonely. To find myself confined without transport, without phones, without shops, without anywhere to go, not knowing anyone, alone.

My hardship really began the morning after I arrived; although eight months pregnant, I had to walk two miles to the nearest shop and two miles back. As it came near the time of my delivery I would begin to panic each night after the last bus had gone, because, without a phone or transport, I didn't know how I would get to the Rotunda Hospital which was ten miles away. The roads had no lights and you'd never see a taxi. But we were hopeful, a new town would be built in two years and the scenery was beautiful.'

After I left each morning that's all Annette had to help her pass the day, the expectation of a new town and the scenery. But two years after our third child Robert was born, Annette became involved in voluntary community work and for the rest of her life this was a huge part of who Annette was.

Here's Annette again: 'As there was no community centres or halls built within the housing estates it left women in very vulnerable positions, especially in winter time. There was nowhere people could meet each other, except knock on someone's door, but as people were strangers it was hard to know who you could trust. Most of the women felt isolated and alone, some more than others, but because we were young and had no one to talk to about it, we thought there must be something wrong with us, and put a brave face on it and covered it up. I remember speaking to a woman one day who was smiling and looked the picture of happiness. The next day I heard she had been taken into St. Loman's suffering from an overdose. This happened a lot. Most women survived the overdose. Unfortunately some didn't, and sadly this is still a fact of life in Tallaght today, so unbearable is the isolation and lack of facilities for women.'

This is what motivated Annette to get involved in community activities, to improve the lot of women in the concrete jungle Tallaght then was. Annette worked ceaselessly to improve the conditions of women in particular, but she could also see that men needed help as well. She never discriminated between men and women in her advocacy when seeking funds and facilities for Tallaght. This is the world we had moved into in 1973, a world that Annette was determined to change for the betterment of all. When Robert was about two years old, Annette got involved with Tallaght Welfare Society which was the start of over 30 years of working tirelessly for the community. During that time she was instrumental in setting up Tallaght Women's Contact Centre and the Women's Awareness Group and she pushed hard for the formation of Tallaght partnership which brought badly needed funds to Tallaght. She also at this time composed a song, *A Song for Tallaght*, which was included on a promotional video for the "Get Tallaght Working" organisation and later another song promoting investment in Tallaght *Tallaght stand up*. In recognition of her work for the community Annette was named Tallaght Person of the year in 1991. It was the year she outlined her definition of what to her defined community and community living and what she aspired to and was working for.

Annette again: 'If I were to write an account of my seventeen years in Tallaght it would take a book not an essay, and maybe some day I will write a book. I believe the future of Tallaght lies with its people. Community for me now means living in common with the people around me. Sharing the same transport, breathing the same air, not always agreeing, feeling the same classism and oppression, hating the same inequalities and injustices, sharing the laughter, the joy, the humour, seeing the good and the bad days. Living in common, twenty-four hours a day, three hundred and sixty five days a year. Physically, socially, recreationally, emotionally, feeling the heartache at seeing the kids emigrate when you know they have the potential but have to leave the shagging country to realise it. Feeling anger at seeing them exploited at part-time employment at low wages. Feeling the despair at seeing them sign on the labour. Feeling the hopelessness and powerlessness at seeing the cycle repeated. Wondering sometimes if the years of words and action have made one bit of difference. Knowing that they have.'

Annette did make a difference. She made life better for so many people, Annette made so many women aware of their potential, their value and the skills they had, but above all, made them feel like women, proud of their femininity and unafraid to be strong enough to step forward to take their place as equals in the community. I can best sum up her contribution to the community, and to women in particular by repeating what one woman said of her after her passing: "She was a woman who spoke for every woman."

I hope by now I have given you an idea of the magnitude of my loss, the huge gap that has been left in my life, in the lives of David, Gina, Robert and the incalculable loss our grandchildren have suffered by not having the love, wisdom and guidance of their Nana as they grow to maturity in a very harsh and hostile world.

Back in 1973, Annette was still waiting to give birth to our third child Robert. I can't remember too much about Robert's birth, I vaguely remember waiting at the bus stop on the Old Blessington Road, on a sunny afternoon in October with Annette and the other two in a double pram. We went into town, leaving David and Gina with my mother and I brought Annette over to the Rotunda. In 1973 the system still was no husbands allowed at the birth, so I would have done what I did with the other two and handed Annette over to a nurse to be taken up to the ward, in the old lift with the sliding gate. I do know that Robert was born in the early hours of the following morning, Tuesday October 16th.What I remember most vividly about Robert's birth is the following night, Wednesday, 17th October. Having come back to Tallaght after visiting Annette in the Rotunda I fed David and put him to bed. I then sat in the kitchen where we had the black and white TV and, with Gina in my arms screaming crying, I tried to watch the England v Poland World Cup soccer match. It was the famous game in which the Polish goalkeeper Thomashanskie, described by Brian Clough as a "clown" knocked England out of the World Cup, I enjoyed the circus as Gina screamed all night.

Our lives became pretty routine for a few years after Robert's birth. With three young children to provide for, on one average wage, life was not a bed of roses, and we lost a bit of the passion that had made the first years of our marriage so memorable. Looking back on those years now, like the England and Poland game, they seemed to be lived in black and white, with not too much happening apart from the mundane. Naturally with three children under four we did not want any more for a while so we began practicing birth control again, but this time there seemed to be less need for it than previously. It's probably in those years, the years of struggle, trying to provide for a young family with limited resources that a lot of marriages flounder. For a while ours was in danger of sinking in a sea of boredom and indifference. I was working late a lot of the time, simply to get enough money to make things that bit more comfortable and I also got involved in trade union activity in IMP which sometimes necessitated late evening meetings. Annette was busy with the children and after a long tiring day for both of us, we were exhausted by the time evening came around. We were not too interested in stimulating conversations, with the result that we drifted a bit. I can't say with any degree of certainty how long this situation lasted but I do know that for a while even our lovemaking suffered. It was perfunctory and routine, not the spontaneous combustions it had previously been.

Somehow or other we got through this negative period and Annette, when David started school and Gina playschool, got involved with Tallaght Welfare Society. This reignited the spark in her which in turn renewed my interest in this newly vibrant and interesting woman.

The Seventies continued uneventfully. Annette got more involved with community activities but with all her involvement and commitment she always managed to put her family first, and never once was there cause for complaint that she was showing the slightest neglect of me or the children. After the period of drifting we got back to something like what our marriage was in the beginning and our love for each other was never in doubt. We also once more, gradually lost interest in birth control and reverted to a normal sex life, but Annette never gave birth again though she did we believe have a miscarriage when Robert was about two.

As the Seventies gave way to the Eighties and Ireland went into recession I lost my job in IMP in 1981 due to the place closing down. I had been there eleven years by this time and got a fairly good redundancy package, six and a half weeks per year which after tax and all other deductions amounted to just over £6000. We had only been abroad twice since our honeymoon in 1968. In 1971 when Annette was pregnant with Gina we went to Majorca for a week with our friends Jimmy and Gretta Morley and on our tenth anniversary in 1978 we'd taken the children to Lloret-de-mar and stayed in the Santa Rosa hotel where we spent our honeymoon. So reverting to our carefree style of years past, and putting the search for a new job on the back-burner, we booked a holiday in Torremolinos with my redundancy money.

I could continue on in this vein, chronicling our life year by year, but I think it would be boring. We did, and encountered the things most normal families do and encounter, the children grew up, made their Communion and Confirmation, left school, went to work, or not as was the case. We had weddings; my brother's and Annette's sisters. We were confronted by sadness; my parents died in the Eighties and Nineties, and our aunts and uncles died. Sickness befell us from time to time, but nothing serious, all the usual things that fill the lives of most families, and we had rows. So from here on I'll concentrate on the things that mostly concerned Annette and me and detach ourselves from other distractions.

CHAPTER FOURTEEN

After I lost my job in IMP in 1981, I worked at various part-time and short-term jobs, including the tote with the racing board, making and selling jewellery with my brother, and as a night operative with a yogurt manufacturing company. Then in 1984, I got a job as sales cashier with HB ice cream. This period in our lives was probably the most affluent and happiest of our marriage so far, though it also included the most serious and marriage threatening incident we ever encountered.

I worked at whatever I could get from 1981 to 1984 with the result that the money, though smaller, did not stop coming in, and it was expertly managed by Annette. We managed to stay out of serious debt, so when I started with HB, on a reasonably good wage we were able to take the family on a holiday to France the following year. A most enjoyable holiday marred only by having to return from Cherbourg and sail into the teeth of hurricane Charlie. This necessitated me spending 30 hours on my back in the overcrowded lounge of the ship, unable to stand, as every time I did so I got violently sick. "Charlie" had no effect whatsoever on the children, who played, ate, and discoed through the storm. They got a great laugh at seeing their Dad prostrate on the floor of the ship, unable to move. While Annette was not in the best of condition she was able keep an eye on the children as they enjoyed the hurricane.

The following year was the start of what was to become our love affair with County Kerry. We took a rail/bus rambler holiday sans the children. It took us first to Ballina in Mayo to visit friends of ours, Brian and Winnie Leonard. I had worked with Brian in Neasden Distributors and kept in touch with him for a while after. We then went to County Clare and from there to Killarney. Both of us were captivated by the beauty of the countryside and the mountains and stayed the rest of our holiday in Killarney. We hired bikes and cycled for days,

*The first photo we ever
had taken together
August 1965*

*The early days of our courtship,
Phoenix Park*

Outside Annette's house
in Ballyfermot

Our first dress dance,
1965

Our wedding day 24th September 1968

On the roof of the Santa Rosa Hotel on our honeymoon

As nomads in Donegal / After the caravan crash

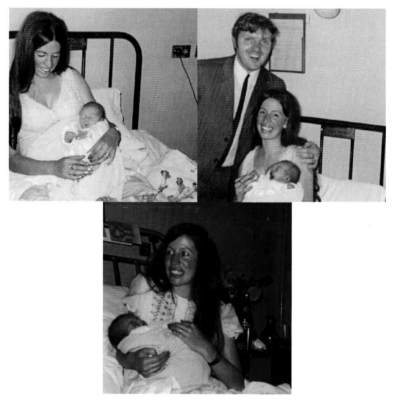

The babies, David, Gina and Robert

President Robinson presents Annette with the Tallaght Person of the year award watched by Patricia Bryan 1991

Annette celebrating winning with some of her friends

British Ambassador, Mr. David Blatherwick (centre) with his wife Clare (left), present a cheque for £1500 to Annette Halpin for Tallaght womens contact centre.

Hosting the British Ambassador and his wife

With friends in Porto Colom

Annette in Dingle

Our mobile home in Dingle

With Carol and Tim Green and Ann and Tony Leggit in France 2004

Gina in France 2004

all around the lakes and grounds of the national park, in the process falling in love with the county and its people.

The following year friends of ours were getting married the day before we were due to commence our holiday again without the children, in a rented house in Waterville, County Kerry. As they had not made any definite plans for a honeymoon we invited them to come with us. We all shared the house for a few days before they headed off on their own. Like the holiday we'd had with our mothers-in-law some years earlier, it was somewhat unorthodox but enjoyable. After Johnny and Ann left, and because Annette felt a bit uncomfortable in the rented house when we learned the owner had died a short time before we arrived and also it was a fair bit outside the village of Waterville, we booked into the Bay View Hotel in Waterville. It was a lovely comfortable hotel and we had a room facing the sea. We loved Waterville and cycled all around the area each day. In the evenings we relaxed in the local pubs and restaurants, enjoying meals in the Huntsman, the Lobster Pot and the Smugglers Inn. We enjoyed it so much that we went back for the next four or five years and all this time our love deepened.

Those holidays became a big feature of our lives and something we looked forward to every year. It was an opportunity for us to be alone together, away from the tensions of our everyday lives. This was particularly true for Annette who was now very deeply involved in community activities and all the stress, emotional heartache and frustrations it brought her. She had a total commitment to alleviate the hardship and burden of others. Annette worked tirelessly for those she saw as less fortunate than her. Her actions were spurred on by her genuine desire to be involved with the community and to help in any way she could, and also her deeply held Christian faith. So when holiday time came around, Annette was more than ready to cast off her everyday cares for a while and relax and rejuvenate herself for what was ahead when she returned. Later in her life Annette composed a song *When the summer comes around again* in which she expressed her joy at what holidays meant to her. The times we spent together on holiday brought us closer together as a couple. We were able to relax totally in each other's company and enjoy the expressions of love and intimacy we could indulge in.

As Annette got more deeply involved in community work she began to compose songs based on what she saw going on around her. She had, from time to time, tried her hand at writing songs before as she was always interested in music. But then, using what she was learning and experiencing as a community worker, she began composing songs with social comment, songs like *Mr. Community welfare officer* a satire on the social welfare system and its disregard for the dignity of people who are in need of help; *Mary's life* a sad parable about a young girl she knew for whom the system proved too much; and *Two miles down* about the effects of unemployment on the young. Listening to those songs now, in this new recession, they could have been composed today. Things are just the same for many people now as they were back when Annette composed them all those years ago.

Apart from songs with social commentary, Annette composed "normal" songs. One in particular became hugely popular with her women friends and indeed with most people who heard her sing it. *I need somebody to love me when I'm down* is a country and western type song about the need for love in our lives. She was called upon to sing it at many a party and function we attended. Annette also composed a, as yet unproduced, musical based on the life of St. Patrick. The music from this became very popular with the choir in our local church, St. Marks, and some of the music is performed at Mass every St. Patrick's Day.

It was also the music I chose to be played at Annette's funeral. I don't want this to become a hagiography, but I do want to record the fact that Annette was a hugely talented composer, and I thankfully have a collection of her songs on a CD to prove it. None of Annette's songs have ever been recorded commercially, which is a mystery to me because they are certainly good enough. Music was a big part of our life and we loved all kinds of music. There was many a night I remember just sitting in with Annette, listening to the Three Tenors, whom she loved, and enjoying a bottle of wine. That's what I miss most now, the quiet nights of intimacy and togetherness that developed between us over the years, with no need to talk, just to be together. The looks, the touch, the silent communication as we sat together on the couch, with Annette's head resting on my shoulder as I gently stroked her hair and face; knowing that each of us was happy and content just being in each other's company.

All that is gone now, the nights in with a glass of wine, the walk to the Plaza or the Belgard for a drink and a chat, the little things we took for granted and that gave us such pleasure, like the trips to Glendalough and the waterworks in Bohernabreena, simple pleasures, but all just a sad and distant memory now. They are receding with each passing day into the haze of memories that comprise the life we've lived, with me fighting hard to retain them and relive them. I try to somehow bring Annette back to be once more by my side, to hold her hand and to hear her voice, to relive what Annette used to describe as "our happy times"; times that are no more. They are the times that I can only relive by retreating into the recesses of my memory and meeting up again with Annette as I conjure up her image, her beautiful smiling face, in the misty haze of what was our past. This I do all the time, praying and wishing that somehow my hopes and prayers will be answered and I will be with Annette again, to relive "our happy times" once more.

CHAPTER FIFTEEN

After our daughter Gina left school in 1989 she went to England to work as a nanny for an Irish family. But the following year Claire, the child she was minding, died. This affected Gina very much as she had nursed her for months and become very attached to her. Gina came home after Claire died and got a job in an office in Tallaght but found it hard to settle into a 9 - 5 situation. She gave up the job after about a year or so and went travelling again, this time to America. After coming home from the States for a while Gina then went to work in a hotel in Badenville, in the Black Forest area of Germany. Annette, Robert and I went over for a holiday in the summer.

We stayed for four days in the hotel Gina was working in and we were very well looked after. Myself and Annette were given a suite and Robert a room overlooking the forest. After our four days of luxurious living we came back to what we were more used to when we moved on to Switzerland, Lake Lucerne to be precise, and stayed for ten days in a caravan on a camp site beside the lake. It was a great holiday, with great weather, which, while we loved Waterville, whetted our appetite for more holidays in sunny locations. Gina came down to visit us for a day or two before we went home. We all went for a boat trip on the lake and went to the top of Mount Pilatus, where some of the James Bond film *Moonraker* was shot. Gina came home for another while at the end of the season before packing her bags again, this time for Australia and Vietnam where she remained for over a year. She returned just after my mother passed away in November 1996.

In 1991 Annette's hard work for the community was recognised and rewarded when she was nominated for an award at the Tallaght Person of the Year ceremony. It came as a huge surprise to Annette when she was invited to the ceremony as a nominee for the award. She was amazed that anyone took the slightest notice of what she did, in what she saw as, the hidden life of the less fortunate in the community.

On the night of the awards we went to the ceremony simply to have a good night out as Annette really did not expect to win. Indeed she was terrified at the thought of winning as she would be expected to make some kind of speech. We were sitting with friends of Annette, the friends who had nominated her for the award in fact. The mood at the table, in everyone except Annette, was one of huge confidence. They were sure that she would be called on to accept the award from the guest of honour, the President of Ireland, Mary Robinson. As the night went on and people relaxed with the help of a few drinks the mood lightened and there was a lot of banter and laughter about the various nominees and the merit of their respective entitlement to the award. But then the time of the presentations came and all chatter stopped.

The nominees for the various categories were called out and the awards distributed. Annette had been nominated for community work, but when the winner of that award was called it was not Annette, at which point I think Annette was happy and began to relax. As she had not won anything Annette thought she was not a contender for the main award, Tallaght Person of the Year 1991. As President Robinson stood beside the chairman of the community council, Annette could not have been more relaxed as she waited for the winner to be announced. Then Patricia Bryan, standing beside President Robinson, opened the envelope, she moved closer to the mike and to a tumultuous roar, simply said: "Annette Halpin."

Annette was too shocked to stand up. She was engulfed by her friends at the table and from others stampeding across the hall. President Robinson had to wait a while before Annette was extracted from the crowds around her and brought to the stage to accept her well earned and deserved award. And incidentally she made a great speech of acceptance, highlighting the needs of Tallaght and its people.

While all this commotion was going on I ran to a phone in the hall and rang Annette's sisters in Ballyfermot with the news and they immediately made their way over to Tallaght to join in the celebrations. I then ran the short distance from St. Mark's GAA club home to waken Gina and Robert (David was not there) with the news and they also came to join the celebrations. What followed was probably the most joyous night the Tallaght Person of the Year awards ever witnessed. We danced until the early hours of the morning, before going home in a state of euphoria.

The next morning Annette proudly began her term as Tallaght Person of the Year by accepting the warm good wishes of our neighbours, some of whom called with a bouquet for her. In my opinion Annette became the quintessential holder of that office as she attended functions all over the area, many of them with me one step behind. To each event she brought her unique charm, grace and beauty, her interest in people and their doings. Most of all she brought her calm dignity and sense of occasion that gave to each event she attended an air of prestige and importance, to her and to those organising the event.

Annette also Internationalised the position by having the courage to host the British Ambassador in Tallaght at a time when trouble was still at boiling point in the North. She paid a return visit to the British embassy for the Queen of England's birthday celebrations later that year, at which party I distinguished myself by drinking for Ireland. It was a great year for Tallaght to have such a worthy and deserving person to represent the community. No one deserved it more.

CHAPTER SIXTEEN

After many years holidaying in Waterville the weather got to us, and in 1996, the year my mother died, we went to Minorca for a week. This was our first taste of all-inclusive holidays, and we loved it. It rekindled our taste for sun holidays and we came home determined to take more. That holiday was in September and in November my mother died. After the rather tentative start to the relationship between my mother and Annette, by the time she died, my mother and Annette were like mother and daughter. My mother told Annette things about our family she never told me. Indeed I learned quite a lot about my extended family from Annette.

When we came back from that holiday my mother and Annette had an afternoon out together in the Royal Dublin hotel at which my mother, maybe conscious of the fact she did not have a lot of time left, told Annette her life story. Many of the things she told her I did not know, nor I suspect did my brother. Annette told me later that she was filled with admiration and love for my mother when she learned of the hard and sometimes sad life she had lived. I think my mother saw in Annette the daughter she never had and Annette was more than happy to be that daughter. My mother's death hit us all hard but none harder than Annette, who that Christmas did not want to celebrate at all. She felt we should not ask anyone into the house as we normally did at Christmas time. Only now, as I am writing this, and recollecting the relationship that developed between them, am I beginning to understand the reason for what happened on the night of my mother's twelfth anniversary, November 2nd, 2008, in the Plaza hotel Tallaght, shortly before Annette's illness became apparent. I will be saying much more about that strange night and the events that followed later.

After the holiday in Minorca travel played a big part in our lives and over the remaining time we spent together we travelled quite a lot. We went to Italy a few times as well as Malta, Austria,

Cyprus, Tunisia, South America, Alaska, and Canada. We also had one memorable trip to the Holy Land in October 2000

That trip to the Holy Land came at a time we were having the most serious problem of our marriage, a problem caused by me on a holiday to Majorca in 1998. As I stated previously we experienced all-inclusive holidays for the first time in Minorca in 1996. We liked them so much that the next year we sought out an all-adult resort, the Los Palomas hotel in Porto Colome Majorca, and we had a fantastic time there. We became closer than ever and met some very nice people that we socialised with and Annette really relaxed. So much so, that some nights when we came back to our room, which was on a corner of the top floor, facing the sea and not overlooked by any other buildings or balconies we made love on the balcony, under the stars. We slept on the balcony, wrapped in each others arms, covered only by a light sheet. After two weeks we truly were reluctant to go home as we were more in love than we had ever been and resented having to share our life with anyone else. We were no sooner back in Dublin than we booked the Los Palomas for our holidays the following year, 1998, the year of our thirtieth wedding anniversary. The year our marriage nearly came to an end.

Over the thirty years of our marriage we had had disagreements and rows, but nothing too serious. We were always able to kiss and make up after a short period of feeling miserable over hurting each other. But what happened in Majorca in 1998 was in a different league to anything that had happened in the past. This time I disrespected, hurt and betrayed Annette in a way I had never done before, in a way that I was, and still am deeply ashamed of. It took its toll on our marriage for years after and was only completely healed during our trip to the Holy Land in 2000.

We had had a great first week in Porto Colome, taking up where we left off and making full use of the balcony. We had requested the same room so everything was going perfectly; we even met some people from the previous year. Then, as the first week came to an end, my eyes betrayed Annette. I really don't know how to put this down, how to say it. It's still a source of huge embarrassment to me and a source of sadness that I hurt Annette the way I did. Here goes, as we were having our lunch on the Saturday of the first week I got up to go to the buffet for something and as I did so, I saw a girl in her late twenties enter the room. She was wearing a green summer dress, with no sleeves and white sandals. I was taken by her appearance and looked at her as she crossed the room, possibly looked at her too long, unaware that Annette was looking at me. I went back to the table and Annette said nothing at this point.

Over the course of the next couple of days I saw this girl again, and without thinking, and to a large extent without being aware of it, I let my eyes linger too long, unaware that Annette was watching me all the time. Like all men I'm sure I have looked at pretty girls before but for some reason I took an unhealthy interest in this girl. It was something I had never done before as I truly loved Annette and never at any time in our relationship or marriage was I, or had I any desire to be, unfaithful. After three days of this carry on, I was standing on the balcony with a pair of binoculars and I am ashamed to say I had them focused on this girl as she was sunbathing by the pool. Annette came out of the room and stood beside me and asked what I was looking at. I of course said nothing in particular, that I was just scanning the horizon and the sea. Annette knew differently and in a fit of tears and anger told me she knew who I was looking at as she had been observing me for the past few days and I could not take my eyes off this young girl.

I was frozen on the spot with shock and shame and at first denied any such thing, but I knew she was right. My mind went into a spin of confusion and shame when it suddenly hit me that I had been behaving like a schoolboy at the first sight of the female body. I'm not sure exactly what happened next, but Annette threw herself on the bed, crying bitter tears which pained me to see as I was the cause of them. All through our marriage I hated to see Annette cry, particularly if I was the cause of those tears, and I had been from time to time, but never for something as hurtful as this. Through her tears Annette questioned her attractiveness, asking me was I now, after thirty years of marriage, finding young girls more attractive and desirable than the mother of my children, the woman who had given me the best years of her life. She reminded me that she had been a young, attractive girl once and now felt old and unwanted. She also said she felt disrespected and insulted that I should behave the way I had in her presence. That she thought at first I was just having a harmless glance at an attractive girl, but as my behaviour went on for days she was angry at the way I was behaving and felt insulted that I did not know or care that she was observing me.

As these words spoken through her tears hit me, I was reduced to tears at what I had done and the hurt I had caused Annette. I truly did not realise I was behaving in such an abominable manner. I never had, nor would I ever, purposely hurt Annette and I tried to tell her so. I apologised for my behaviour and told her she was the only one for me and I loved her and thought she was the most beautiful woman I had ever seen in my life, and I meant every word of it. But the damage was done. I had behaved like a fool, and in the process hurt, badly hurt, the woman I loved. I can't explain my behaviour over those few days because I was unaware I was doing anything wrong. We had been on sun holidays before where I had seen attractive young girls in various states of undress, including topless, and I had never behaved in such a way nor felt any desire to do so, but for some reason, I had, on this occasion behaved like a complete idiot.

My apology did not cut any ice with Annette as she felt betrayed and nothing I said could stop the tears. Her tears penetrated my heart and I would have done anything in my power to undo the hurt I had caused her. Maybe what I did would not be such a big issue for some people, but because of the depth of love and trust we had invested in our marriage, and the closeness we felt, it was a huge breach of trust on my part and a huge feeling of betrayal for Annette, and I knew that.

We somehow got through the rest of the week but I'm sure the other people must have wondered about the change of mood, which was decidedly sombre. And whenever possible we avoided socialising. What should have been a very happy occasion for us became a nightmare for me as I'm sure it must have been for Annette too. I tried to make amends for what I had done but nothing helped. She went into a frame of mind and a mood I had never seen her in before. She was silent and withdrawn, with me and everyone else. I was so sorry for what I had done; I was also very ashamed and tried to tell Annette so, but it was as if I was talking to a wall.

The rest of the second week was agony for both of us and it could not end soon enough. We spoke very little on the way home and I was afraid of what would happen when we did get home; would our children notice the difference in our behaviour and how would we explain it? But fair dues to Annette, when we got home I immediately noticed she perked up a bit and tried to give the impression that everything was normal. I continued trying to tell her how sorry I was and how ashamed I felt about what had happened but she seemed to be numb to my entreaties. I did not blame her one bit as I knew I was one hundred per cent responsible for the gulf that was now between us and I never stopped telling her how sorry I was and how much I loved her.

When we did talk about the incident from time to time, usually early on weekend mornings as we lay in bed together, Annette spoke with sadness about what we'd had and how she now felt she could not trust me anymore. Hearing those words hurt me badly, because I knew what I had lost and I was afraid I was going to lose much more. I was terrified I was going to lose Annette. But I was not going to let that happen. I begged Annette to forgive me; I swore my fidelity and my love to her and promised I would never again behave in such a way as I had done in Majorca. Annette was slow to accept my pleadings and I, for a time, thought our marriage was at an end. But gradually Annette's attitude changed. She began to believe I was truly remorseful about what had happened but our relationship was still a long way from what it had been before we went to Majorca and I clearly still had a lot of convincing to do before it would be like that again, if ever.

It has been extremely hard, embarrassing and painful for me to write what I have just written, but I promised Annette when I told her I was going to do this memoir, and asked her to help me do it, that I would be totally honest in what I wrote and that I would include this painful episode. To have left it out would be a distortion of our marriage. It did happen, so I have tried to put it down as accurately as I remember it. To do otherwise would be to disrespect Annette and her perspective of our marriage, and I would never do that again.

After all the happiness and love we had enjoyed in our relationship up to then, it was a very painful time we were then entering into and one I found very difficult to cope with. In spite of what had happened Annette never withdrew from me sexually and we never stopped making love but it was not the same. Our lovemaking had always been spontaneous and passionate, and fun. But now things were very tentative, with a sense of just going through the motions. I knew that if we were to get through this, and I do believe that after a while Annette began to believe I was truly remorseful about what I had done and was trying to forgive me, then we had to continue making love, because if that stopped then there was no way back for us. Both of us I believe knew that, but while Annette always participated fully when we did make love the fun and passion was not there any more.

I tried really hard to make Annette see how sorry I was, and how much I wanted things to be as they once were between us, but I knew I had hurt Annette badly and it would not be easy to get back to what our life had been like before. Both of us tried to act as normal as possible when the children were around and I don't think they noticed anything unusual in our behaviour, likewise with our friends and family. But we needed to be alone together more if we were to resolve the situation.

After a few months, Annette wanted to talk more and more about what I had done and why. I tried to explain as best I could, but as I did not fully know why myself, it was hard to explain it to Annette. It was a painful experience being confronted with my behaviour time after time and asked to explain it. I felt ashamed and embarrassed in front of Annette as I tried to rationalise what I had done. What I did know and what I continued to tell Annette was that I loved only her, and how sorry I was for my actions in Majorca. We talked and talked it through, over and over again, and while Annette wanted to be forgiving, as was her nature, she was finding it hard to fully trust me, hard to give herself as completely as she had done, because she was afraid of getting hurt again. We needed extended time alone together to resolve and repair the damage that had been caused to our marriage. Annette wanted to believe and forgive me; she did not want us to break up because of this incident, but she did not know if she could ever be as close and loving with me again, as she said "the trust was broken." We had to try to rekindle the fire that was now only a smouldering ember. As long as that spark was there, and it was, there was always the chance of starting the fire again. We had been together for thirty years now and I was not prepared to give up all that we had experienced together and all the love we had bestowed on each other in that time without a fight. The loss, measured against what we had, was too great a price to pay for what would, in reality, have been for most other couples a misdemeanour. But because our love was so strong and all encompassing, because the degree of trust had been absolute, what I did was all the more shocking and hurtful to Annette. It shattered the trust she had unreservedly invested in me and in our marriage and she was hurt and disillusioned by what I had done. In spite of all that I knew there was still a strong bond holding us together and now that we both wanted our marriage to continue I was prepared to do whatever it took to reignite the flames I had so nearly extinguished.

Chapter Seventeen

It was at this time we got the chance to buy a mobile home in Dingle, County Kerry. And it was in Dingle that the trust and passion began to come back into our marriage again. It was Annette's idea to look for a mobile home as a getaway for ourselves, so we'd be alone to work through our difficulties. We had somewhere nearer than Dingle in mind, but after putting an ad in *Buy and Sell* magazine the price requested for mobile homes on the east coast was way beyond what we could afford to pay and it looked like a mobile home was a non-starter.

Then, when we had all but forgotten about it, we got a call from a man in Dingle out of the blue one day. He wanted to know if we were still looking for a mobile home. Annette was not home when the call came, but I took the details and after explaining that we had been looking for somewhere nearer Dublin I promised to speak to my wife and get back to him. Later that evening when Annette came home I told her about the call and the mobile in Dingle. Like me, her first reaction was, Dingle was too far, especially as neither of us then drove a car. I had never been to Dingle, but Annette had been there once with her sister Caroline at some weekend conference some years before and liked it. After talking some more about it, and in view of the fact that we were unlikely to be able to afford one near Dublin, we decided that we would ring the man back and get more details. This we did, and to cut a long story short we decided we would go down the following weekend and have a look at the mobile.

The weekend we picked turned out to be one of the best weekends of the year weather wise. We were met at Tralee train station by Paul Scanlon, the owner of the mobile, who took great pride in bringing us over the Conor Pass and into Dingle town. Dingle looked magnificent, with clear blue water in the bay, surrounded by green hills which swept down to the sea. After having a drive around the town Paul then took us to Bin

Bann to see the mobile. It was an old mobile which had been used by Paul's daughter Pauline but she had moved out and the mobile was now vacant. It was situated in a side garden beside Paul's house, but with a high fence and ample space between the mobile and the house, and it had a small garden of its own. It was on a hill overlooking Dingle Bay, and from it we could see the "Fungi" boats as they brought visitors on trips to see Fungi, the Dingle Bay dolphin. Although old, the mobile was in pretty good condition, and Paul had installed running water and electricity, as well as a flush toilet. It had two bedrooms, a galley kitchen and a large living area. It was exactly what we were looking for, and the price was right too. The only problem was the distance from Dublin. It would take the best part of a day to get down to Dingle. We really liked what we saw and would have bought it there and then if it had been nearer to Dublin.

We did not make a decision that day but told Paul that we would have to think about it for a day or so as it really was a long journey from Dublin. We enjoyed the rest of the weekend in Dingle and took a trip on the boats to see Fungi. While we were on the boat we could see the mobile nestling on the hill overlooking the bay. We did not know what to do about the mobile; the distance was the only stumbling block.

After a day or so we knew we had to make a decision and let Paul know what we were going to do. We sat down one night and weighed up all the options and decided it was worth taking a chance on. So we rang Paul the next day and said we would take it. It was the beginning of October and we told Paul we would be down in a week or so to take possession of our 'new' mobile.

Annette had not yet started to drive so we had to get the train to Tralee and a bus from there to Dingle. As the mobile was in Bin Bann, which is about one and a half miles from Dingle, we had to get off the bus at the race course corner, near Ballintaggart House. We then walked with our haversacks, down the side of the racecourse and up the hill to Paul's house and the mobile. The weather was not as kind to us as it had been the first time we came to Dingle. It was more like the Dingle weather we came to know so well in the years ahead, breezy and raining.

By the time we got to the mobile we were wet through and through and were beginning to have second thoughts about the decision we had made. I'm pretty sure if the weather had been like this when we came to view the mobile we would not have bought it. But then we would have missed so much. Eileen, Paul's wife was there when we reached the mobile. We had not met her before as she was in Dublin with her sister the first time we came down. I don't know what Paul had told her about the people who had bought the mobile in her garden, but I got the impression she was expecting someone younger, not a couple in their fifties. How and ever we got the keys and moved our wet haversacks and ourselves into our new holiday home.

The first thing Annette always did when we entered somewhere new, even hotel rooms, was to bless the place with holy water, so as to protect and guard us against all harm, and this she proceeded to do with the mobile. It must have worked, because for the next ten years we felt nothing but good in that old mobile. The time we spent there over the years brought us back together even closer and with a greater depth of love than we had ever had. But it did not happen all at once. Annette was still hurting, and I still had a lot of making up to do. But it started that wet October weekend in Dingle, as we made the first tentative efforts to get back to where we had been last May, before we went to Majorca.

We spent three days in Dingle that first time and set the pattern for what we would do in the future there. After getting out of our wet clothes, we changed and made a cup of coffee in our new home from home, sorted out our clothes and bedding and, as the rain had then stopped for a while, set off to walk into town. Over the years this was something Annette loved to do the first day we arrived, get into the mobile, have a cup of coffee, get changed and sort out our gear and if it was not raining ,walk down to Maura de Barra's which, some years later was to become John Benny's, for a meal. Then we'd relax and listen to the music until late and get a taxi back to the mobile. It was these simple little routines that helped us break down the barriers that had come between us, and reawaken the love that was so nearly destroyed by my juvenile behaviour in Majorca.

As we got ready to go home that October weekend, I won't say our problems had been resolved, but I think it is fair to say we had made a good start. (I'm getting vibes from Annette agreeing with me on this)

We did not go down to Dingle again that year, not until the St. Patrick's week of 1999, but after coming home in October I felt a bit more hopeful that we could get back to what we'd had before. The chemistry was still there between us, even if the reaction of the elements was just a little bit slower in the emission of light.

CHAPTER EIGHTEEN

Shortly after Christmas 1998 I took a big risk; without telling or consulting with Annette, I booked a holiday in the Las Palomas Hotel Porto Colome, and requested the same room we had been in the previous two years. I knew in my heart and soul this had the makings of a major disaster, but I truly felt that if we were to get over the problem between us, we, and particularly I, had to face it head on. We had spent and enjoyed three great weeks in Las Palomas and one which had been a nightmare. I really believed we had to exorcise that nightmare before we could make real progress, to go back face our demons and slay them.

When I told Annette what I had done I was surprised by her reaction. I had expected I would have to justify and defend my actions, but Annette was philosophical about it and if I remember correctly only said something like, "do you think that's a good idea?" And when I said I did, she simply replied "we'll see."

Before we went on holiday to Majorca we were in Dingle about three times for varying lengths of time, from three days to almost a week. And each time we went down things got better, to the extent that on at least one occasion Annette initiated the love making. We had never stopped making love but needless to say sometimes it was not great. But in Dingle we did become closer again and enjoyed being in bed together in that snug little bedroom in the mobile.

Being alone together in Dingle allowed us to talk about the year before without the fear of being interrupted, and Annette spelled it out to me in no uncertain way how hurt and humiliated she had felt by my action, which in turn hurt and humiliated me. We talked a lot and Annette got rid of a lot of the anger she felt towards me. I let her talk and took it square on the chin. I was really hurt by some of the things she said, but I know she needed to say them, and I was more hurt because of the obvious pain I had caused her. This was something that had to be done; Annette had to get rid of her anger and I had to listen to it and take it on the chin. We could not have done this at home as we would not have had sufficient time alone, and also we were able to let the tears flow freely knowing nobody was going to see us in a distressed state. If only for the opportunity of talking and crying our way back together, Dingle was worth buying. At every opportunity I told Annette how much I loved her and how sorry I was for my behaviour, in the hope that if I said it often enough she would begin to believe me and know what I did in Porto Colome was a once off and would never happen again.

When the time came for us to go to Majorca I was less fearful than I had been when I booked the holiday. I had spent the last year wooing Annette as if I was only going out with her again, and she was beginning to see and know how remorseful I was about the way I had hurt her. Still this would be a huge challenge for us both and there was a bit of tension when it came time to go. When we reached the hotel I did feel a little tense and apprehensive, remembering how it was when we were last there, but Annette seemed quite relaxed and unperturbed.

We checked in and got the keys to our room, 517 I think was the number. The same top corner room we'd had before. After unpacking our clothes I did not dare to go out on the balcony as I would normally have done, but Annette did. When I showed no sign of joining her she called me and told me to come out. I went out and rather nervously held Annette's hand as we looked out over the magnificent vista of the Mediterranean which was before us. After a few moments Annette turned to me and said "we'll be all right" and I knew then I had made the right decision in coming back to Porto Colome. While I had never stopped telling Annette I loved her, Annette's expression of love for me was a bit watered down. I know she wanted to love me as she had in the past, but found it difficult to do so because of the hurt I had caused her and her fear that something might happen again if she loved me as unconditionally as she had in the past. I have not the slightest doubt that Annette never stopped loving me, but I also know it was for a time difficult for her to do so.

But as we held hands on the balcony in the Los Palomas Annette looked at me and said "I love you" and I knew she once more meant it as much as she had in the past, before all the turmoil of the past year had caused us both such heartache. The risk had been worth taking as we had a great holiday, and the events of the year before did not cast a shadow over our third visit.

After a few days of good food and wine and rest and relaxation, we were as comfortable as we ever had been together. We were soon making use of the balcony for outdoor recreation again. We went back to Porto Colome one more time after that because I felt we had to put a distance between the nightmare week and the more recent happy memories. And it worked; we relaxed and enjoyed all the resort had to offer. Anyone seeing us there that fourth time would never have guessed how big a part that little corner of Majorca had played in our lives and how close our thirty year marriage had been to ending there. It was saved because we both knew we had something worth saving, and worked hard to do so.

Those two years, 1998 - 2000, were tough years for us and had we not had Dingle to escape to from time to time I'm not sure I would be writing this memoir now; our story could have been very different. Dingle gave us the space to confront our problem head on, away from our family and let the anger and tears flow freely, particularly the tears, which washed away the hurt and exposed the love that was always there and nourished it's growth again so that the second phase of our life together was even more loving, caring and passionate than the first. So much so that Annette wrote a song for me in 2001 *Since I started loving you baby* which summed up our new relationship and her love for me.

We had begun our journey back to where we were prior to June 1998 in Dingle but in June 2000 we were not quite there just yet. There was still a residue of sadness with Annette that it had happened at all. From time to time she told me that "stuff" was still an issue with her. Now it was her who was telling me she loved me and wanted to rid herself of this "stuff" that was coming up from time to time, causing her to question the love she felt for me. I had done all I could do and said all I could say to Annette to let her know how sorry I was and how deeply I loved her, and I knew at this point that she believed me, but there was still one final hurdle to get over in our new relationship, and that was cleared when we got the chance to renew our marriage vows. We, in effect, got married again, in Cana of Galilee on 16th October, 2000, during our trip to the Holy Land. That was the end of the nightmare that started in Majorca in 1998 and could so easily have resulted in us parting, but the love that had been forged over the previous thirty years proved to be stronger than the betrayal that threatened to tear us apart.

We were now in a new marriage and the events of 1998 were never mentioned again. Both of us threw ourselves into it with as much enthusiasm and passion as we had into our first marriage. For the next nine years we loved each other even more than we had thought it possible for any two people to love.

That holiday in the Holy Land was memorable for more than our second wedding. It happened at the start of the Intifada which was precipitated by Ariel Sharon going on a visit to the temple mount in Jerusalem in September which upset the Palestinians. When it was time for us to go in October the fighting had started and there was a question as to whether we should or could go. Eventually, after a delay of six or seven hours at Dublin airport while the insurance implications of travelling to Israel at this time were explained to us most of the group booked to go went. A few decided not to go and had their luggage removed from the plane. The rest of us boarded the El-Al flight for Tel-Aviv.

The first few days of the trip went without a hitch, but then the day we were due to visit the tomb of King David and the Wailing Wall all hell broke lose. Two Israeli soldiers were taken hostage and killed in a house in Gaza. Their bodies were thrown from the window onto the street below. This infuriated the Israelis who decided to close the crossing on the road from Jerusalem, where we were at the time, and Bethlehem, where our hotel was. The tour guide, who was Palestinian, was informed of the situation and immediately said we would have to leave the tomb of King David and forgo our planned visit to the Wailing Wall so we could get back to the hotel in Bethlehem before the crossings were closed.

As we made our way back to our hotel we had to take a diversion off the main road as we encountered a battle between the Israelis and the Palestinians at a spot inside the Palestinian-controlled sector known as Rachel's Tomb. Although this was inside the PLO controlled area, the tomb was sacred to the Israelis and the military maintained a presence there all the time. They came in and out by helicopter while under fire from the PLO. The diversion took us through what was in effect a housing estate on high ground, looking down on Rachel's Tomb. As the bus made its way through the housing estate it came to a roundabout which was above the tomb. From some of the houses beside the roundabout PLO gunmen were firing at the tomb. The gunmen motioned to the driver to drive around the roundabout, and as he did so some of them used the bus as cover to get nearer to the tomb. For a few moments, until we cleared the roundabout we were in danger of being shot as the soldiers in the tomb returned fire at the gunmen firing from the cover of the bus. We managed to get back to the hotel unharmed but for a while the situation did not look too good for us, and at that point many of us questioned the wisdom of going on this trip at all.

That night as we were having dinner we could hear the sound of battle outside the hotel. The Israeli army attacked the Palestinians who had erected barricades around their enclaves in the city. This went on for hours until near midnight when the sound of the shooting stopped. At this stage Annette and most of the others had gone to a convent beside the hotel to pray and I could not resist the temptation to venture out of the hotel and take a walk around the now silent and barricaded streets which were still manned by heavily-armed militia. My every move was watched, but I was not impeded at all. Annette and the others returned to the hotel before I got back and when Annette asked where I was, she was told by a hotel employee exactly where I was at that moment.

Although I was free to walk the streets I was monitored all the way. As I walked around Bethlehem that night the thought struck me that it must have been like this in Ireland during the Civil War, as it was reminiscent of old photographs I had seen of that period of our history with militia men manning makeshift barricades at street corners.

Next day things had returned to what passed for normal in Bethlehem, by that I mean the Israelis had withdrawn from the area controlled by the Palestinians. They were still out in force patrolling the streets with rifles and machine guns. The tour guide decided it was safe for the tour to continue so we set off in our bus for a trip to the Dead Sea.

After a lovely day spent floating in the salt waters of the Dead Sea and a visit to Qumran, the site of the Dead Sea Scrolls, we started back to our hotel. The positions of the Israelis and the PLO had hardened by this time and we found ourselves caught in the middle. When we came to the position controlled by the Israelis on the Jerusalem/Bethlehem road, the Israelis did not want to let us pass through. After pleading that we were an Irish group of tourists, with no part to play in the conflict and nowhere to go to in Jerusalem as our hotel was in Bethlehem they let us through. The relief we felt about getting through was soon shattered when we came to the PLO position at the other end of the road. The PLO guards at the crossing decided that the Israelis were not the ones who would get to say who got into the area they controlled. They refused to let us through to our hotel in Bethlehem. Again we pleaded that we were Irish but it made no difference as the PLO guards pointed their guns at the guide and driver and told them to turn the bus and go back to Jerusalem. We went back to the Israeli' controlled crossing in the hope of getting some sort of accommodation in Jerusalem but the Israeli attitude was the same as the PLO – they would decide who entered Jerusalem, not the PLO. So we were sent back to the other end of the road again.

After two more trips up and down the Jerusalem/Bethlehem road and been refused admission to either city we were in no man's land and night was fast approaching. At this point the

Irish tour company representative phoned the Irish Embassy or Consulate which I think was in Jerusalem and the Ambassador was on the case very quickly. We had another wait of about an hour and then he came and spoke to us. By this time we were hungry and annoyed at the treatment that had been meted out by both sides in the conflict. After heated exchanges it was made clear to the Ambassador that we wanted to get back to our hotel and get something to eat, that we'd had enough 'tooing and froing' up and down the road.

The Ambassador spoke to the PLO guards and explained our position, that we were only a group of pilgrims in their country who sympathised with their cause but they were doing that cause no good by the way we were being treated. After prolonged discussions we were eventually allowed through. But relief at being allowed to return to our hotel soon turned to fear as we reached it. Darkness had fallen as we disembarked from the bus, tired and hungry after our ordeal on the road. But as we entered the hotel we were met by heavily-armed PLO soldiers. They had taken over the hotel to get the food which they said they wanted for the people of Bethlehem because the Israelis had blocked supplies reaching the city. As we were marshalled into the foyer of the hotel by armed soldiers we were told by one of the leaders of the PLO we would not be harmed, but we could not stay in the hotel any longer. We were given one hour to pack and vacate the hotel.

Personally I did not need an hour. I took Annette's arm and led her up to our room and as she packed, I tried to ring the *Irish Independent* in Dublin. I was hoping I could make a few pounds by letting them have an exclusive story from the frontline of battle. Alas my exclusive never reached the front page as the PLO had cut the phone lines.

In less, far less than the hour we had been given we were all back in the bus ready to go, to where we did not know. The militants did not allow us to have a meal before we were sent on our way, but they did allow the hotel staff, who were very upset at the way we were being treated, to give us water for our journey. So after taking a few crates of bottled water aboard the bus and saying goodbye to the hotel staff we left Bethlehem and drove into the night. When we were a sufficient distance from the hotel the guide stopped the bus and told us we were going to Tiberias in the north of the country. Tiberias was on the itinerary of the tour, but we were not due there for another day or so. As we had not eaten, the guide explained that we would stop at a shop and get some bread, cold meat and anything else that was available and eat on the way.

Outside the city of Jerusalem we stopped at a delicatessen and got our supplies, and then we had one of the most wonderful experiences of the holiday. We drove into the hills overlooking the city of Jerusalem and in a clearing which gave us a spectacular view of the city by night, we had a midnight picnic. Jerusalem was spread out like a sea of twinkling lights below us. If there was ever a time and place to sing that anthem "Jerusalem, Jerusalem" this was it, and we did.

We reached Tiberias after an all night drive across the desert and in the early hours of the morning reached our hotel and luckily the hotel was ready for us. The rest of the holiday, after all the excitement we had experienced, was quite normal and we encountered no more hostility.

From Tiberias we went to Cana, and during the course of the visit we got the opportunity to renew our marriage vows. We had been told before we left Tiberias that this might be possible, but it was not certain. The unrest in the country meant things tended to change quite suddenly. This was an unexpected turn, renewing our marriage vows, and one we had not anticipated. But when it was mentioned I asked Annette would she like to do it. She did not hesitate and said she would. After a visit to the market in Tiberias and a walk around the town and places of interest we were brought to the wedding sanctuary. We entered the church and had an introductory talk by a priest on the history of the sanctuary and the area. He then said he would officiate at a short ceremony to renew the marriage vows of any couples who wished to do so. Without a moment's hesitation, I grabbed Annette's hand and almost pulled her from the church pew up to the altar, ahead of everyone else. Compared to the last time we'd exchanged marriage vows the dress style was somewhat different, instead of long white dresses, veils and elaborate hairstyles, it was very casual. Annette wore a sari type wrap around skirt over shorts which she had been wearing, she brought this skirt with her for use when visiting churches, a yellow t-shirt, sandals and a brightly coloured silk stole which she put over her head during the ceremony. I was dressed in a blue t-shirt, light grey trousers and light slip on shoes.

I think about eight or nine couples took vows that day, all with their own particular reason for doing so. But thirty-two years after taking our first vows I was determined to prove that old Sinatra classic right: "love is lovelier the second time around" and so it turned out to be. More loving, more passionate, more caring and probably most important of all, we became closer, much closer than we had ever been, two truly did become one. And we were much more considerate of the feelings of each other. When we came out of the church we bought a few bottles of Cana wedding wine and that night toasted our new beginning.

Two days after taking our vows we left Tel Aviv for Dublin, a different couple from the one that had departed ten days earlier. We were once more Andy and Annette, the young lovers from the Sixties.

When we arrived into Dublin airport to our surprise we were met by a group of reporters, wanting to question us about our adventure in the Holy Land. That night in the *Evening Herald* there was a big picture of Annette and me, with the caption "Pilgrims of Terror". It is now hanging on the wall at home. But for us the real story of that holiday was not the fact that we had come under fire from the warring factions, been terrorised and sent packing at gun point from our hotel. It was that we had put our problems behind us for good and were once more as madly in love as we had been at the start of our marriage.

The new millennium was a good time for marriage in the Halpin household, over the next few years all our children got married and fled the coup, leaving the two "newly-weds" free to be as luvvie dovey as they liked, and we were. Things could not have been better. Annette started driving and set up a little business working from home as a personal development and community development consultant. She was putting all the knowledge and experience she had gained while working in the community in Tallaght to good use. And when she started driving, principally because I was too lazy to do so, we were able to get down to Dingle quicker and more often.

Besides being a great place for us, Dingle also proved to be a blessing for Annette's mother Mary. Unfortunately in the early 2000s Mary started showing symptoms of dementia. This resulted in her not being able to go on sun holidays with her women friends, something she had done for years and loved. So Annette took her to Dingle for a week each year and she loved it down there, relaxing on the beach at Bin Bann and listening to the music in the bars in town at night.

Just one last mention of our troubles in Majorca – later on when we could laugh about it, and we did, Annette told me that she had learned that the girl was a lesbian.

Chapter Nineteen

It was around this time that Annette started to learn to drive. She started with a car jointly owned by herself and Gina. Unfortunately Gina wrote that car off, by skidding on black ice on the Lucan Road one St. Stephan's Day. She was very lucky and wasn't injured and Annette then got herself a little red Citroën AX which she loved to drive. We made many a trip to Dingle in that car. In 2004, Annette drove that little Citroën in the country of its origin, France.

Dingle was still a firm favourite with us and now that Annette was driving it was that much easier to get there, with no more lugging heavy haversacks and bags on train and bus journeys. We just threw the bedding into the back of the car and headed off, footloose and fancy free. They were good times for us, and Annette loved the freedom of the mobile. As she used to say, it was clutter free, not like home.

By this time Annette had also started her own business as a community consultant. At last she was getting paid for a job she had been doing for years for nothing. But Annette being Annette, she felt odd charging groups for her services and advice because she had been giving it all for free for so long. She very often charged less than the rate she was entitled to charge if she felt the group did not have much money or was deserving of her time and experience. As a result of this habit she never made as much money as she could have made had she been less sensitive to the needs of others. In reality her business was little more than a hobby she enjoyed which earned her pocket money. She was happy with that, as money had never been a motivating factor for Annette, which was just as well for me as I never had very much money. She just wanted to help those she felt could benefit from her experience and improve their position in life. In this regard she felt very much for those she believed were marginalised or discriminated against in society and enjoyed working with groups such as the Traveller women' s groups whom she had a great respect for. Indeed she composed a song, *"Everyone"* which, after it was performed by a Traveller choir at her memorial show after her passing became very popular with Travellers thanks to its promotion by Fr. Derek Farrell ,who is the Parish Priest to the Traveller Parish and a good friend of Annette's

Our trips to Dingle became very important to us as we could be truly ourselves down there. As Annette wrote in one of her songs: 'it doesn't matter if the Sun don't shine, if it doesn't shine most of the time, I'll be happy just sitting, and singing with the one I love.'

That's exactly the way it was for us in Dingle, rain or shine, it didn't matter. Some of the most pleasurable moments we spent there were when we were holding each other in the little double bed, as the candles Annette always lit in the bedroom flickered, their flame heating the perfumed oils which filled the room with a pleasant aroma, while the rain beat out a tattoo on the tin roof of the mobile. As I write these words I can visualise the scene through my tears, the loss of such moments is heart-breaking. That's what Dingle meant to us, a place where we could let our passions run free and be one in body and soul.

There was also the more simple and public pleasures that we indulged in. We took great pleasure walking into town and having a meal in Maura de Barra's (later John Benny Moriarty's) on the evening of our arrival. We made a point of having a meal in a more upmarket restaurant as well on one night of our stay. In this way we came across The Global Village, which became a favourite of ours, and as we became familiar faces there, we were always made very welcome by Nuala and her staff.

In our first year in Dingle we had bought two second-hand bikes in Foxey Johns and used them to cycle all around the area. Annette loved to cycle to Ventry and walk on the beach and then have refreshments in the Ventry Inn, looking out at the sea. One fine day we cycled all around the Slea Head scenic route, stopping at Ballyferriter and the beach from *Ryan's Daughter* along the way. At night we loved to listen to the music of Eoin Duignan, John Browne or Michael O'Herliahy or indeed any of the great musicians who played in Maria de Barras/John Benny's or the Droichead Beag, which were the places we usually went to.

Our time in Dingle is something I often think about now, and, if I was a praying person, I would thank God for it, because at the time it came to us, it truly was a godsend. Over the ten years we were there our love reached depths (maybe heights is more appropriate) of emotion I did not think possible. But those times are gone now and I won't be keeping the mobile after this year. I'll go down once or twice more to cry alone for the loss I have suffered. I'll look into the little bedroom and remember our happy times. And just maybe if I wish hard enough the veil of time will lift and I'll see once more, two lovers lost in a passionate embrace.

Dingle is over for me now. The mobile served its purpose; we could not have asked for more from that old *"Bohan"*. It more than gave value for the price we paid for it. In fact it was priceless, and I'm so glad now we took the chance and made the long journey from Dublin to Dingle, because in reality that journey was part of the journey of our life and love which started in Bray in 1965. I could not stand the pain and the loneliness of being in Dingle without Annette. Dingle was somewhere we found ourselves again, I would be lost if I went there alone.

In 2002 I lost my job in HB ice cream after almost nineteen years when the place closed. The van sales section in which I'd worked was franchised out to another company. I was not too concerned as I was then gone fifty-seven years of age and was getting tired of work anyway. I was able to avail of a fairly good redundancy/early retirement package which included a pension, so money was not a big problem particularly as all the children were now self-sufficient. As a matter of fact, David and Robert were no longer living at home and Gina only intermittently. Annette was also still earning a bit from her consultancy work.

With the redundancy money we planned to travel a bit and to also spend more time in Dingle. That year we went to Dingle for the Dingle Races as well as a few more times when Annette had no work on. Later in the year, near Christmas we went to Lake Garda in Italy. It was a trip we thoroughly enjoyed as the town of Riva was bedecked with Christmas lights and was like something out of a fairy tale. We stayed at the Hotel Liberty and met some very nice people. We took trips to Venice and Verona where we visited the alleged home of Juliet. I risked life and limb to climb the wall of the house and leave a love letter to Annette, as was the custom of lovers to ensure lasting love. I was never going to be complacent about our relationship again and was ready to accept help from all sources to make sure it continued, especially from such famous lovers as Romeo and Juliet.

Retirement suited me and I relaxed into it quite easily and not for one moment did I miss the monotony of the daily chore of work. I always had liked cooking, so after Christmas 2002 I enrolled in a catering course run by Cert and learned a few new recipes which I tried out on Annette. Unfortunately Annette, as in so many other ways, was very conservative when it came to food and did not appreciate my adventurous style of cooking, so I ended up putting on weight as I finished what Annette left on her plate, I could not get enough of my own cooking.

Our relationship continued on an upward trajectory into 2003. We planned another holiday to Italy for June, after our son Robert got married. For the past year or so Robert had been living with his girlfriend Fiona Farrell in a house they had bought on the other side of Tallaght. After the wedding which was celebrated in the Green Isle Hotel we set off for Italy, visiting Naples, Sorrento, San Giovanni and Capri. Again things could not have been better and we enjoyed our time together, particularly when we found a lovely open air bar and restaurant in Sorrento with a little dance band. It was very reminiscent of the old Shangri-La, all those years ago in Dalkey. Every night after dinner in our hotel we were very anti-social and slipped away from the group we were with to be on our own. We danced under the stars in the warm Italian night air until midnight. When the band put away their instruments we strolled back to our hotel, arm in arm, to enjoy a night cap with any of our group who were still up. And not content with that, we usually had another night cap on our balcony when we got back to our room, and I do mean an alcoholic night cap, as this particular balcony was quite small and was overlooked.

Chapter Twenty

Coming up to Christmas 2003 I saw an advertisement in a newspaper looking for "mature couriers" to work on a holiday camp in France for the 2004 season. My noticing this ad was to lead us into one of the happiest periods of our life together. I showed the ad to Annette and asked her would she be interested in applying for the job. I was still unemployed but Annette was still doing some consultancy work on a part-time basis. If we got this job it would necessitate her dropping her job for a while. It would not be a major problem as most of the groups Annette worked with broke up for the summer anyway, and there would be very little work between the end of May and the middle of September, which basically was the holiday season in France. After a short discussion we decided to apply for the job. A few days after Christmas we were invited to attend an interview in the Ormonde Hotel near Capel Street.

We went to the interview and learned the job was on a caravan park somewhere in France, the exact location would not be divulged until we got there as the company, Kelair travel, also known as Campotel, had a number of sites, stretching from Brittany to Biarritz in the south of France. After training in a camp in Les Sables d'Olonne in the Vendee region sites would be allocated. We were easy with that as no matter where we were sent it would all be new to us and we did not know one site from another anyway.

A short time after the interview we were informed we were successful and the training would start in the middle of May for a camp opening on the 5th of June. We accepted the position and proceeded to inform our family and friends of our plans for the summer. Some of them thought we were mad setting off on such a venture at our age, but more of them admired our courage and wished they had the nerve to do such a thing themselves. We'd always liked doing something different and looked forward to the experience. There was only one niggling little worry.

Annette had not been driving for long and had only recently passed her driving test, so the prospect of driving in France on the "wrong" side of the road and negotiating roundabouts from the "wrong" side was a bit of a concern. But fair dues to her, she was prepared to give it a go.

We had a big surprise before we left for France when Gina told us she was pregnant. She had been seeing a fellow for a while but we did not think it was anything serious, she had been with fellows before and nothing came of it. But this was obviously different. With this news Annette became a bit anxious about going to France as she felt she should be there for Gina. I think she was remembering her own pregnancy with David and the fact that her own mother had to go back to work after the death of her father. But Gina insisted that we go to France. Anyway she wanted to move back into our house to save on rent so that she and her boyfriend David could save for the house they were hoping to buy. The fact that we were going to France was perfect timing for her and before we went she had moved back home.

Around the middle of May we packed our bags and headed down to Rosslare to catch the ferry to Cherbourg. We embarked on our new careers as "mature couriers" to, we hoped, mature holiday-makers somewhere in France.

On the ship we met up with another couple who were also going to work for Kelair and who had been in France before. As the male of this couple, whose names I now do not remember, had driven in France before it was agreed that we would let them lead the way.

We reached Cherbourg the following evening and decided that rather than starting to drive into the night we would stay in a B&B and set off early the next morning. At about nine o'clock the next morning Annette sat behind the wheel of her red Citroën, with me beside her. I had a map of France spread out on my lap, as she intoned a prayer for divine help on our journey. We set off across France without knowing where our final destination was going to be.

As we drove along behind our leaders, I was trying to keep tabs on where we were according to the map on my lap. After we'd been driving for an hour or so the names of the towns and villages on my map differed from the places we were passing through. I did not say anything to Annette at first, but as we continued to drive past and through places that were not on the map I had to say something. I told Annette that the places we were passing through were not on the route we were supposed to be taking. She would not believe me. She said I was reading the map incorrectly, that the other couple had been here before and knew the way.

For the next while I continued to ask Annette to signal the couple in front to stop, so we could check the map, but to no avail as Annette felt I was wrong. That is until we came upon a road sign pointing to Le Havre which was in the opposite direction to where we should have been going. At this point I insisted that Annette signal the other couple to stop. They had also noticed the sign for Le Havre and were in the process of stopping anyway.

We checked the map and found we had taken a wrong turn at a roundabout shortly after leaving Cherbourg which set us in a completely different direction to where we should have being going. We had been driving for about three hours in the wrong direction, a great start to our time in France. We spent the next fifteen minutes trying to decide how best to get back on track before coming to the conclusion that we only had one option. We would have to drive across the country towards Rennes and get on the motorway to Nantes and from there to Les Sables D'Olonne. We had estimated a journey time of about six or seven hours from Cherbourg but now that was going to be considerably longer. Our worry was that we would not get to the camp outside Les Sables D'Olonne before dark.

We drove like the hammers of hell, and, fair dues to Annette, she passed her introduction to driving on the Continent with flying colours. She joked later that because the car was French it knew the roads and all she had to do was hold onto the wheel. It was a pity it did not know the roads when we left Cherbourg.

After a hectic day's driving we made the camp, shortly before ten that night. We were just in time to get into a local restaurant where a table had been reserved for us by Kelair, when we had contacted them during the day and told them of our predicament. After a very long and tiring day, especially for Annette, we were only too happy to sit down and sample real French cooking for the first time, all washed down with a couple of bottles of good red wine.

The next day we started our training. It consisted of learning how to clean barbecues, put on duvets and clean mobile homes, so nothing new there. After a week or so of this we were allocated our site for the season. We were sent to Camp le Littoral which was just on the other side of Les Sables, near Port Bourgenay. It was a really lovely camp site, in a lovely location, right on the coast as the name suggested.

The time we spent in Le Littoral near Sables d'Olonne was one of the happiest periods of our life. We were like teenagers again. The freedom was exhilarating and we made full use of it. After an initial period of hard work, while we got the chalets ready for clients, we had a lot of spare time as we only had ten chalets to look after. We also met and became friends with two other "mature" couples on the site who were working for other holiday companies. Carol and Tim Green and Ann and Tony Leggit became firm friends over the four month season. We enjoyed some great nights together when we drank and sang well into the night. On one occasion we had to be asked to be quiet by the clients in the chalets as we, "the mature couriers," were keeping the paying customers awake. Annette had brought her guitar and she became a very popular turn at these courier get-together sessions. From time-to-time we were joined by some of the clients who found our brand of entertainment preferable to what was on offer in the camp bar. Indeed one night, near the end of the season, Gasper, the owner of the camp site and his partner Annloue came across to our pitch which was directly across from the camp bar. They joined in the fun and stayed until the early hours of the morning.

Ann Leggit used to sing a beautiful song at these sessions that I never heard before or since, it was called *Something in Red*. Annette and I used to love to hear her sing it.

Our sojourn in Le Littoral was more like a long holiday, with the occasional bit of work now and then. We had a lot of free time once we got the clients settled in so during the day we often went to the beach near Port Bourgenay, Plage du Veillion. It was a very safe and sandy beach, and I loved to see how great Annette looked in her bikini sunbathing. At home she was very conscious of exposing herself in public places, even in a swimsuit, but in France she was much more relaxed and confident about it. But I wanted more, and I used to pester her to go topless on the beach when there were few people around. On one or two occasions she acceded to my request which made my day.

Other times Annette drove us to the surrounding towns to visit the churches and markets. It was a real tonic for us to be so free of the everyday chores we had to contend with at home. It gave us a chance to live like carefree teenagers in our mature years, which I now believe is the best time to act like carefree teenagers. You have all the experience and none of the inhibitions of youth and you certainly have none of the hang-ups that were so restricting for us when we were teenagers growing up in the Ireland of the late Fifties and early Sixties.

We were free of all the care, worry and responsibility for anyone but ourselves. And I think we each saw a new side to the person we had shared the last thirty-five years with. I became much more sociable and less inhibited with people which pleased Annette immensely. She put away her sense of "decorum" and became much lighter in her behaviour, like topless sunbathing, which she would never do at home. The sense of freedom was great and with no bills to pay, we irresponsibly spent everything we earned, and more besides, on the good life. It really was a liberating experience for us and we took full advantage of it. We became even closer and more in love as a result.

Of course working in such close proximity every day was not without its moments of friction. One of the things I found out about Annette during our working days was that she was a perfectionist when it came to cleaning the chalets. My attitude was, let's get in and out as quickly as possible, so we would have more free time, but Annette believed in cleaning every nook and cranny in the chalet, and at times under the chalet. She would not leave until she was one hundred per cent happy that every last cup, saucer, plate and piece of cutlery was sparkling clean, because, as she said, that's the way she would like to find the place if she was coming on holidays. At times this infuriated me, as I, after finishing my part of the work, had to stand and wait in the scorching heat, sweating, as Annette went over and over the cups, saucers and pots, making sure there was not a mark on them. On a few occasions our voices were raised as high as the temperature as we argued our points. But we usually ended up laughing as we stood facing each other, in our sweaty t-shirts, with our hair stuck to our heads. We were pretty dirty to boot after spending the morning cleaning chalets and barbeques. Then we'd kiss and make up, put the cleaning materials into our little hand cart and head back to our caravan for a shower, a light lunch and a glass of wine. Afterwards we would either head somewhere off site like Talmont or Saint-Gilles-Croix-De-Vie for the afternoon or else sit by the pool with a cool drink if we felt lazy.

It was a great time to be a "mature teenager" and pretend we had no responsibilities at home in Ireland, but we had responsibilities and we thought about them from time to time. Annette's mother Mary, was getting progressively worse with dementia at this time and Annette did feel guilty about leaving the care of her mother to her sisters and brother at home; and our daughter Gina was pregnant, unmarried and at home without her parents. From time to time these things did make us feel that having such a good time was irresponsible and that we should have been at home fulfilling our roles as parents and daughter and son-in-law. But I'm glad to say those moments passed quickly, and we reverted to our summer roles as middle-aged, good-timers pretty quickly. We convinced ourselves that there would be plenty of time to revert to our more responsible roles when we got home, and that the time spent away would make us more capable of coping with the situation. When we said it often enough it worked, and we did not feel too guilty as we resumed our mid-life hiatus of pleasure.

We had a brief return to the role of responsible parents in August when Gina, then five months pregnant, came to stay with us for a week. We prepared the small bedroom in the caravan for her and took down all the erotic pictures we had on the walls (caught ya, only joking!). Gina was supposed to fly from Dublin to Paris and then get the train to Les Sables d'Olonne where we would pick her up, but because of delays in Paris the train she eventually got only went as far as La Roche-Sur-Yon. This was about sixty miles from Le Littoral. We were expecting clients that night who were late arriving, so after waiting as long as we could for them we had to ask Ann and Tony to cover for us. Annette then had to drive the sixty miles to pick Gina up.

Again Annette rose to the occasion. As darkness began to fall she ventured out on the French roads to pick up our daughter. We got to Le Roche-Sur-Yon just in time to meet Gina as she came out of the train station. It was dark and late when we got back to Le Sables, but we managed to find a restaurant that was still open and we had a meal before we went back to the camp.

Annette was delighted to see Gina looking so well in her pregnancy, as was I. She had a lovely relaxing week with us, mostly sitting and reading by the pool, which I'm sure did her the world of good. It was just what she needed at that time. We took great pride in introducing her to our friends on the site and she joined us for dinner and drinks each night. On those nights her parents were on their best behaviour. We went for a few trips to towns along the coast on the days we were free and all the sea air could not but have done her good. Her stay also did us good. We did not stay out as late when she was with us, and the week allowed us to recharge our batteries for the rest of the season, which we needed to do at that stage.

At the end of the week we left Gina to the train station in Le Sables, and with tears in our eyes, waved her off on her journey to Paris and home. It had been a very good week which we thoroughly enjoyed. Seeing Gina in her pregnant condition made us long for the time to return home and be with her when our grandchild was born. But before that we had four or five weeks left to use up and to get rid of our irresponsible behaviour. We had to purge ourselves of the carefree lifestyle that was in danger of becoming ingrained in our systems. The weather, after a slight blip for a few days in August was beautiful again and we spent as much time as we could on the beach in Port Bourgenay by day. At night we went into Le Sables, Jard-Sur-Mer or Le Trench-Sur-Mer for meals with Carol and Tim or Tony and Ann.

On Annette's birthday, the 13th of August, we went out on our own to Port Bourgenay to a lovely little restaurant, Le Manureva. We had seen it earlier and we had a very romantic and intimate meal there together. I remember we reflected on how lucky we were to have this time together at this stage of our lives. I'm in tears as I write this and would give anything for that time with Annette again.

After dinner we took a stroll on the beach and then came back to get a taxi, but none were available. We decided to walk back along the coastal walk which was skirted by a forest. By this time it was almost dark, but as we had walked the path many times by day, we were confident we would have no trouble finding our way back to the camp. How different things look in the dark. We started walking through the not very dense woods. A hundred yards or so later we should have been on the coastal walk, with the camp straight ahead. But after fifteen minutes we were still in the woods, and it was now completely dark. I know we were not exactly lost in a wilderness, miles from anywhere and we were certainly not in mortal danger, but nevertheless it was unnerving to have lost our bearings. We did not know which direction we were headed in as we had made a few turns thinking we were going out of the woods. After walking around for a few more minutes we still could not find our way out. We stopped talking and stood silently listening for the sound of the sea. After a few moments of total silence we could hear the faintest lapping of waves and we headed in that direction. As we very carefully made our way forward, the sound got progressively more wavelike. We finally exited the woods onto the coastal path. We were facing the bright lights of La Sables in the distance and a few minutes later we were back in the camp. We made it to the bar in time for a celebratory drink with our friends for Annette's birthday.

We truly had a wonderful time in France that year. Annette was never happier than when she was cycling to Mass on a fine sunny evening, with the summer wind blowing in her hair and her arms and legs exposed to the evening sun, as it deepened the already golden tan on her smooth skin. Although Annette was then fifty-eight years of age, to my admiring eyes, as she cycled off to Mass in the little church near Port Bourgenay on those summer evenings, she was still the young and beautiful girl of eighteen I had been lucky enough to meet in Bray all those years before; only now she was my wife, and the woman I held tight in bed every night. As Deano sings: "how lucky can one guy be."

We learned a lot about the Irish on holiday during our time in France. Some of it was not anything to be proud of, but this is not the time or place to go down that road. We did our job as best we could and we were always conscious that our clients had paid a lot of money for the privilege of staying in a chalet for a few weeks, so we, and particularly Annette, went out of our way to be as helpful and informative about the area as we could be. We wanted our clients to have the best time possible. While I did a lot of the heavy work, cleaning the barbeques, changing the gas cylinders and bits of maintenance work, Annette ran the Buzzy Bees children's club. She was a natural at this and the children loved her. She went way beyond what was required or expected of her, organising games and making sure no child was left out of the fun. And occasionally being a "Nana" to a young child left alone by their parents for the first time. Her group of children had so much fun that the girls running the kiddie's clubs for the other holiday companies asked if they could join their group with Annette's.

As all things do, the season came to an end in September. It was suddenly time to pack up and say our goodbyes to the new friends we had made. We had the usual exchange of addresses and promises to keep in touch, and if we were in the vicinity to drop in. But these events are one-off affairs and although we sent Christmas cards we never met again, which is probably as it should be. We had met under particular circumstances when we were all away from our own environment and free to be the people we wanted to be and wanted others to see us as. If we met up again in a more "normal" environment, and I mean this about us all, I'm sure we would not have "gelled" as well as we did in France. In the camp we had no reason to be anything other than person we wanted to be at that moment. We were free to drop our inhibitions and be who we really were. We were like people who don masks and fancy dress costumes at a ball and challenge others to guess who they are. In France we were masquerading as a couple of mature couriers, indulging in a bit of harmless immaturity as we reached back through the years for a brief reprise of our youth. And for four months Annette and I had the privilege of just that, being young again and being responsible only for ourselves, answerable to no one for our behaviour and behaving only to please each other. I think we both liked what we saw. And we continued to like what we saw when we came home.

It really was a source of strength to us to have had that time together. We were no sooner home than Annette got involved in the care of her mother. We took her out of the house to give her sister Louise a break from time to time. Gina was staying in our house in Tallaght while she waited for the baby to be born, and her boyfriend, Dave, now her husband, was there a lot of the time as well. So straight away it was back to being the responsible adults our families expected us to be as normal service resumed. But we did not mind, well not too much. France was a great experience and one we were glad we had taken on. It had opened our eyes so that we saw the person we'd married in a completely new, and dare I say it, sexually attractive way. Things got back to normal pretty quickly though, Annette resumed her part-time consultancy work and I started to look for a job. I was now over two years out of a "real job" and I thought it was time to get back into the workforce before I got much older or I would not get back at all. I had no luck in that department until after Christmas when I got a job counting cash in Securicor in Rialto.

CHAPTER TWENTY ONE

As Christmas approached so did the time of Gina's delivery. We were all looking forward to the new arrival, who we knew would be a boy. Gina ran over her time and had to be taken in to the Rotunda where she had a section. Thankfully everything went well, and on 13th December, Senan O'Toole was born, our first grandchild. Annette immediately introduced him to Mozart to soothe and calm him before bedtime. Gina and Dave stayed with us for another three months before moving into their own apartment in Park West.

If all that was not enough, around the same time our eldest son, David, announced that he and his girlfriend Ciara Byrne, whom he had been living with for the past four years or so, were engaged. They planned to get married the following June. There was no end to the excitement in the Halpin household.

We had our new grandson, Senan, with us for Christmas and his presence added a new dimension to the celebrations. Gina and Dave were delighted with their new son as were we all and Christmas was a very happy occasion.

Shortly after Christmas we were invited to meet Sheena from Kelair to talk about us going back to France that summer. We all met up and, after a chat, we decided we would go back again. To bridge the time until I was due to go back to France I took the job with Securicor.

In early April, Gina, Dave and Senan moved into their new home and we started to get ready for France. We had only been to Dingle a few times the previous year because of our time in France and it looked like it would be the same in 2005. We went down in April and told Paul Scanlon that we would be going back to France again, whereupon he asked if his daughter Pauline, for whom the mobile was originally bought, could use it until we got back, while the house she was buying with her boyfriend was being built. We agreed as the mobile would be lying idle for the summer, as our own children did not want to use it.

A few weeks before we were due to sail to France, I got a phone call from Niall Bergin, the Chief Guide in Kilmainham Jail, with an offer of a job I had not applied for. How this came about was that, over a year before, I had applied for a position as a guide in Rathfarnham Castle. I had attended an interview but I did not get the job. I was, however, put on a panel for future vacancies should one arise. And one had arisen in the Pearse Museum in Rathfarnham. After expressing surprise at this turn of events I told Niall that I was due to go to France in a few weeks and asked for time to consider his offer. He said he would have to know in a matter of a day or two, as if I did not want the job he would offer it to the next person on the panel. Now the strange thing was that a few days before I got the phone call from Niall I had started reading Ruth Dudley Edwards' biography of Patrick Pearse, *The Triumph of Failure* and now, out of the blue, I was being offered a job as tour guide in his old school, St. Enda's.

The job offer presented me with a dilemma. While France had been great the year before, it was only a job for a few months. There was also no guarantee that things would be as good this year, or that we would be with the same people. I told Annette about the phone call and she reminded me that we had told Sheena we would be going back and it was now only a few weeks before we were to sail. She felt we could not pull out now as it would leave Sheena in an awkward position, but I was not listening. I kept thinking how strange it was that I should be offered this job, a job I had not applied for just when I had started reading Pearse's story. We discussed the situation in depth, and after agonising over it for two days, and Annette saying the decision was mine to make, I decided I would take the job in St. Enda's and inform Sheena that we would not be going to France that year.

At the time I made that decision I was only thinking of myself and once again I let Annette down. While I was aware that she was looking forward to going back to France I did not give sufficient weight to her feelings and made the decision purely for my own selfish reasons. It was only after making the decision that I became fully aware of what a disappointment it was to Annette. When she had said the decision was mine, she did not believe that I would pull out of our commitment to Kelair but at the time I felt that I was meant to take the job in St. Enda's because of the, to me, strange circumstances in which it came about.

Anyway the decision was made and I went to work as a tour guide in the Pearse Museum which occupied my summer, while Annette had nowhere to go, as we had also given up the mobile in Dingle. But again Annette showed how strong her love was and how forgiving she was. She supported me all the way in my new job, putting aside her own disappointment and sense of loss at not being given the chance to have another season of freedom.

We learnt later that Carol and Tim did not go back again either and that Ann and Tony did not enjoy their second year as much as the first. Maybe things like that are only meant to be done once and trying to re-create the magic does not always work. Not going to France that year also meant we were there for David and Ciara's wedding, and we did not have to fly home from France for it, which had been our plan. Also Annette's mother's condition got progressively worse that year and she was hospitalised in September. A few months later she was transferred to the nursing home where she is still living at the time of writing.

My time in St. Enda's proved to be a very interesting and happy time. Looking back on it now, I would not have liked to have missed it, as it took in the celebrations commemorating the 90th anniversary of the Easter Rising. I was very proud and honoured to play a small part in those celebrations by conducting tours of the house, including one tour with Fr Joseph Mallin, the son and last surviving next-of-kin of one of the executed leaders, Michael Mallin.

It was while I was in St. Enda's that I started to write. I had written a play after we came back from France called *The*

Day the Commie's came to Town. It was based on an incident that occurred in 1955 when Yugoslavia came to Dublin to play Ireland in a soccer match in Dalymount Park. The game had been objected to by the then Archbishop of Dublin, John Charles McQuaid. In St. Enda's I was inspired to write another play. It turned out to be a very long piece, with a Pearse-like character as the central player. It was written in three parts, the first I called "Remission of Sins", the second "A Nation Once Again", and the third "Unity?". I bundled them all under the title *Mise Eire.* Since then I have written five or six more plays and film scripts, but so far have had only one produced, a cabaret-style show called *Nighthawks, the Musical.* It was based on a famous painting by the American artist Edward Hopper and staged in the Plaza Hotel running during September/ November 2008. I will be writing more about this later, as the strange incident which occurred on the last night of the show marked the beginning of Annette's illness. I worked in St. Enda's until it closed for renovations after the 1916 Commemorations in May 2006. I'd spent a very happy year there.

Chapter Twenty Two

11 a.m. 22nd July, 2009

I want to break the narrative of the story here. It's 11 a.m. on the morning of July 22nd, 2009, my 64th birthday. It is the first time in forty-three years that Annette was not by my side when I woke up on my birthday. The first time she was not there to wish me a happy birthday, with a kiss and a hug. And I am missing that little ritual so much my heart is breaking.

I have just come back from the cemetery where I laid a bunch of fresh flowers on Annette's grave, and watered them with my tears. I am still crying as I write this. The words of the Beatles' song are going around in my mind, "will you still love me will you still need me when I'm 64". I know if she were still here she would, and I certainly love and need Annette now more than I've ever loved or needed her. I need to feel her presence around and near me because everything seems so empty and meaningless without her as I face into the latter part of my existence alone.

I lived for Annette and now that she's not here anymore I just stumble on from one day to the next without giving it much thought. Last night I went to a concert in Vicar Street with Annette's brother Liam, not because I wanted to go, but because Liam thought he was being kind and I went just to please him. That's how it is, I just stumble along and go where I'm asked with no real interest in where I am or who I'm with. My mind is never in the same place as my body, my mind is always thinking of Annette. So it does not matter where I am, only half of me is there.

I'm 64 now and I can see nothing but an empty lonely life ahead of me, at a time when I thought myself and Annette would be relaxing into our latter years together, with the time to travel to new places and enjoy the pleasure of our children and grandchildren. None of those things will happen now. How cruel life can be. Oh I know I have my children and grandchildren, but the part of my life Annette filled, and only now that she is gone am I realising how big a part that was, nothing or nobody can fill or replace. We always celebrated each other's birthday by going out, sometimes only for a few drinks in the Belgard, but no matter what we did, the night was always finished off by us coming home and having a glass of wine and a hug and a kiss on the couch. That's what I'll miss most about this, the first birthday without my beautiful wife, the love of my life, my Annette.

My God it's hard to write this, but I'll keep going. It's over three months since Annette passed away, over three months since I kissed and held her and I miss her more than ever. I want to hold her again, I want to kiss her again, just to touch her. The pain of missing her only gets worse with every passing day, and today it's unbearable. I wish to God this day was over.

I stood at the grave this morning and asked Annette not to forget me, where ever she is now. That's a fear that has been running through my mind for the past few weeks, that she will forget I ever existed, and that thought frightens me. I know it's irrational to think like that, but not having seen or held Annette for so long now and knowing she is still somewhere out there, the thought that she will forget me is tormenting my mind. I want to be with her I can't live without her.

When I broke off the narrative of the story I did not know what I was going to write, only that I wanted to record the fact that this was the first time in forty-three years that we would be apart on one of our birthdays. There was a lot I wanted to say but the words just would not come. Sometimes it's not possible to translate the things that go around in your mind into words on a page, and that's the way it is for me. My mind and thoughts are full of Annette but the words won't move from there onto the page in front of me.

This day will pass as all days do, and tomorrow it won't be my birthday anymore, but I know that the pain of losing Annette will still be there, will always be there, no matter what day it is. I know that the fear I have of being forgotten by her will also be there and will remain with me until I can be with her again, to hold her and caress her and tell her how much I love her.

I hope to God that day won't be too long in coming.

11.15 p.m. 22nd July, 2009

All the family came over to celebrate my birthday and to give me presents. We had a Chinese take-away and tried to be as normal as we could, but there was a huge gap at the table which could not be filled. It was the first time we had got together as a family since Annette passed away, and it was painful. We talked about Annette a lot, which pleased me.

After they all left I cycled up to the cemetery. When I got there I was surprised to see the tombstone had been erected as it had not been there this morning. It looks very well, but was also very shocking, as it confirms, beyond all doubt, that Annette is no longer with us. The final confirmation that she has passed on is now cast in stone for all eternity.

My birthday is almost over and I'm very glad for that. Although the family tried to make a celebration of the day it could never be that for me. How do you celebrate not being with the woman you love? I cried a lot today thinking of other happier birthdays and missing Annette so much, but that's the way it's going to be from now on.

When I came back from the cemetery I rang the family to tell them the tombstone had been erected and Gina immediately said that this was Mam's birthday present to me. I had been very anxious that it would be erected before Annette's birthday, and I was continually reminding the monumental people that it had to be it erected before the 13th of August. Gina said that her Mam had got it erected for my birthday. She could be right.

It's now midnight and the first birthday in forty-three years I've spent without Annette is over. I'm going to bed now, to the big, smelly, empty bed that I'll fill with tears. I hope I'll dream of Annette to night. My heart is breaking trying to live without her, but at least she still remembers me.

The next big hurdle is August 13th, Annette's birthday.

CHAPTER TWENTY THREE

T he year 2006 was the year Annette turned sixty, and the
year she finally got to Brazil. Annette's plans to go to
Brazil when she was in the Legion of Mary had been
scuppered when she married me and I had often said to her over
the years that I would take her there some day, so what better
time than her sixtieth birthday. And because she had to wait so
long I threw in Argentina and Uruguay as well.

This grand tour happened in September 2006, after we had
a big dinner party in the Plaza Hotel for family and friends on
the night of Saturday, 12th August, because her birthday fell on
a Sunday. In the second week in September we headed off to
Buenos Aires via London for our trip to South America. Our
itinerary would take us to Buenos Aires for two days and then
across the River Plate by ferry to the town of Colonia in Uruguay.
After two days in Colonia, which lived up to it's name as a very
colonial type of town, we went to the capital, Montevideo for a
few days, before travelling overland up through the country to
a town called Salto and on to Iguaçu Falls. From there, again
overland, we went up along the coast of Brazil to Rio, stopping
along the way and staying in the beautiful old town of Parati
and on llha Grande, a tropical island off the coast.

We went with a tour company called Gap which catered
for backpackers and stayed in small comfortable hotels and
pensoes. Needless to say we were by far the oldest on the tour,
but we wanted to do it that way. We wanted to see a lot more
of the countries we were in than if we travelled by plane from
destination to destination. The backpacking part of the tour
lasted sixteen days and when we reached Rio, after two days
with the group, we stayed a further six days in a hotel near the
beach on our own.

It was a wonderful experience for us and we fitted in very
well with the younger people on the tour. On our thirty-eight
wedding anniversary, which we spent on the llha Grande, they

surprised us by decorating our cabin with flowers, and inside they covered the bed in roses and left chocolates and wine, with a picture of the island signed by them all, with lovely sentiments and good wishes for our anniversary. We were really surprised and delighted by the gesture and the trouble they had gone to for us. That night we all went to a little bar at the seafront and had a few Caipirinhas.

The holiday was a wonderful experience and we both enjoyed it immensely, but the highlight had to be Rio. What a city. No pictures you will ever see of it do it justice. It has to be the most spectacular setting for a city in the world. The vistas are breathtaking, especially the views from the top of the Corcovado, the statue of Christ the Redeemer. The views have to be seen with the naked eye to go any way to capturing the magnificence of what lies below you.

We did all the usual touristy things, the Sugar Loaf, Copacabana and Ipanema beaches, the Maracana Stadium and the Garota de Ipanema where Antonio Carlos Jobim composed the song *The Girl from Ipanema*. I think for Annette the highlight was when she went to the Favelas, high in the hills above Rio. For a day she did what she had been training to do when I first met her. She went loaded down with gifts and goodies to give to the children who lived in the tin and wooden huts high in the Hills. I did not go to the Favelas with her as I felt that it was something she would prefer to do on her own.

The poverty that lived side-by-side with the wealth in Rio was astonishing, and nobody seemed to take any notice of it. You could be sitting in a restaurant enjoying a steak and across the road a young woman and child or a man might be lying on the pavement, fast asleep. We stayed in a four star hotel near the beach and on the corner there seemed to be a colony of people who lived there. One man in particular seemed to live on a kitchen chair, propped up against the wall. Every day when we went out he was there and when we came back late at night he was still there, sitting on his chair. One thing that struck us about the people of the street was that they never bothered you looking for handouts. Although they were poor they had a great dignity about them.

On the day we visited the Garota de Ipanema I took a photo of Annette as she was walking on the piece of land which separates Ipanema and Copacobana beaches, near Forte de Copacabana. It's a lovely shot of Annette, and it epitomises her to a tee. She is walking with arms swinging loosely by her side, her hair loose, with her sunglasses on top of her head, smiling and carefree, completely at ease and in the open air where she loved to be, with the peaks of Morro Dois Irmãos, Ipanema Beach and the Favelas behind her. I did not know when I took that picture of Annette, that two years later it would be the picture I would choose to be on her memorial card. When I look at it now, Annette is the girl from Ipanema. The beautiful girl Antonio Carlos Jobim composed his famous song about many years ago is personified for me in that photo of Annette.

****

Friday, 24th July, *2009, afternoon.*

I'm going to divert from the narrative again, because I believe I've discovered the meaning of a message that was given to me in the Plaza Hotel on the night of November 2nd, 2008. It was the night of the twelfth anniversary of my mother's death and the night my show "Nighthawks" ended. The content of that message has been puzzling me and the family ever since I was given it. But today I believe that message was fulfilled, and I now know what it meant. I will be writing in detail about that strange night later, but I want to put on record now, that this morning while I was in the cemetery I did something that, as I was doing it, brought that night back into sharp focus, and the words that were spoken to me that night took on a new meaning. I am certain now I know what the message was meant to convey. As most of what was conveyed to me in the Plaza has now come to pass I did something I had been thinking of doing for some time, I contacted the person who gave me the message and I am meeting her next Friday, July 31st. What will transpire at that meeting I have no way of knowing. It may be a complete waste of time, or it may shed more light and give more meaning to Annette's passing, but as events have unfolded I felt it was necessary for me to contact that person again and if possible to get some clarification about what had been said to me in the Plaza in November. If I did not do so I would be forever wondering if there was anything anyone could have done that would have helped Annette, or was her death the preordained end of her journey here on earth.

Since Annette passed away, on a number of occasions I have had what I call "thought intrusions" they are what I can only describe as sudden communications from Annette entering my mind. I will give a few examples. Annette was always on to me about the amount of clutter I gathered in the house and was forever telling me to tidy it up. Before the headstone was erected and the grave tidied up, I had vases of flowers, ornaments from the mobile in Dingle and pictures and candles on it. One day I brought down two small angel figures which had been on the wall at home. As I bent down to put the figures on the grave, I was almost knocked to the ground by the force of a thought intrusion which shot through my mind saying: "you have the grave as cluttered as the house." On another occasion, as I sat in my accustomed position on the couch at home looking at the television, I threw my legs up on the couch to where Annette used to sit. All at once my mind received a thought intrusion, "get your feet off me." Before starting to write this book I stood at the grave one day and told Annette what I was going to do and asked her to help me write it. All at once I could 'hear' shooting through my mind: "I'll be your ghost writer", said in a jocular way.

As I have already mentioned Annette always blessed something new with holy water as soon as she got it and today as I stood at the grave I got a thought intrusion from her to bless the head stone with holy water. This thought came into my mind completely out of the blue when I was thinking of something else.

I will bring holy water with me the next time I visit the cemetery and do what Annette wants.

CHAPTER TWENTY FOUR

We came back from South America to the impending birth of two new grandchildren. Both Gina and Ciara were pregnant and due before Christmas. I also got a job as a sales assistant in Marks and Spencer's supermarket. I was employed in the Dundrum store for training, in anticipation of the Tallaght store opening after Christmas.

The babies were born within a few days of each other. David and Ciara's Mina, was born on Monday, 13th November and Gina and Dave's, Ella May was born on Friday, 17th November.

Annette was delighted with her new granddaughters and could not wait to get to the hospital to see them. That year, for the first time since we had moved to Tallaght, we did not spent Christmas in our own home. Normally we had them all over on Christmas Day, but because the babies were so young David and Ciara wanted to stay at home in Rathvilly, likewise Gina, now that her family had doubled in size, wanted to have a family Christmas in her own house in Celbridge.

Gina and Dave invited Annette and I and Robert and his wife Fiona to dinner on Christmas Day in Celbridge where we had a most enjoyable day with the grandchildren. It was a bit of a break not having to cook a big meal and just sitting down and enjoying it being handed up to you. The only drawback was coming home to a cold house that night.

Things were pretty much routine for a while then. I was working in M&S and Annette was still doing a bit of part-time work, though not a lot. Then shortly after Christmas I drew Annette's attention to a job I had seen advertised in a Sunday paper. It was for a Community Development Worker with South Dublin County Council. The offices of S.D.C.C. were only down the road from us so I suggested to Annette that she should get an application form and apply for the job as she had all the necessary qualifications. Annette thought she would not have a chance of the job because she had not worked in a 'real job' for so long and also she thought she might be too old to be considered. But I persisted in urging her to apply and I think I just might have gone and picked up an application form for her myself.

Annette did apply for the job and after two or three interviews she was offered it on a two year contract, starting on 16th April, 2007. She was very nervous starting, and was afraid she would not be able for it, but once she got into it she loved the job. By all accounts she did very well at the work, and why wouldn't she, hadn't she been doing the same work for years for nothing. The only difference now was she was getting paid for it.

We both took time out from our jobs that summer to go on a holiday to Bulgaria. In my case it turned out to be on a permanent basis as I did not relish working most weekends which were required in M&S. Annette was happy to go back to her job.

With Annette now working full-time I started a phase in our relationship that I got to love. I was cooking Annette's dinner every evening and having it on the table for her when she came in around 5.30 p.m. each evening. From my last experience of home cooking I had learned what not to cook for Annette, so this time the fare was conservative, fish, chicken, fish, chicken more fish, more chicken, and so on. After dinner each evening we developed a routine, we went into the front room, and as we watched the news, with Annette's head resting on my shoulder, we'd fall into a lovely relaxed sleep for about an hour. I'll always remember the smile of contentment on Annette's face when she woke up from those little snoozes.

I miss those times now, how much a part of our lives they had become and how quickly they were taken from us. I 'dine' alone most evenings now, usually on microwave meals, and never fall asleep afterwards as I'm too preoccupied thinking of Annette, and how it used to be. My mind does it's best to conjure up those times again, as I sit on the couch alone looking at Annette's picture over the fireplace and wishing she was with me still. It's the simple things I miss most, just sitting together or holding hands as we went for a walk after our little snooze some nights, or me clearing up as Annette got ready to go to her prayer group meeting on Tuesday nights, or driving over to see Annette's mother in the nursing home, and sometimes stopping at the Belgard to get a bottle of wine on the way home. And then on Friday night, after Annette's week's work was finished, she unwound, put on something comfortable and settled down to watch *The Late Late Show* with a bottle of wine and a snack of some kind. And when it was over we'd put on *Later with Jools Holland* a show Annette loved to watch as she loved music, all kinds of music. Little inconsequential things like that we did without thinking about and took for granted, but now things I would give a king's ransom to be able to do again.

Those evenings were what Annette called our happy times and they were just that,simple, happy times in the company of the person you love have no equal, and no amount of money could ever buy the happiness we knew then.

What we did not know was how soon and how suddenly it was all going to end. One day, that's all it took to upend our lives and forever change the way we lived. And we did not see it coming.

One of the worst things about being alone in the house is eating on my own, particularly breakfast. Breakfast was one of the times I loved most to be with Annette. Right from the start of our marriage we began a habit of having breakfast in bed. When I worked for Neasden Distributors at the very beginning of our marriage I got a large silver hot tray. I used to cook breakfast and bring it into Annette on the tray. I'd get back into bed with her and we'd have breakfast together under the warmth of the sheets. Most mornings, breakfast was only coffee, toast and sometimes an egg. On weekends I'd cook a full breakfast of rashers, sausages and eggs. No matter how early we had to be up, we always made time to have breakfast in bed, and when it was finished a little hug and cuddle, and at weekends something more. It was always hard to get out of bed when Annette was in it. I always thought Annette was at her most beautiful first thing in the morning. Her skin was so soft and relaxed after a night's sleep and her eyes and face looked so serene. I never failed to tell her how much I loved her and how great and sexy she looked first thing in the morning, and I'm so glad now that I did.

Those mornings in bed went a long way to making our marriage as happy and as fulfilling as it was. They went a long way to keeping the spark of love alive between us for so long. Apart from the physical aspect of being in bed together, we also had some great discussions and debates about all kinds of topics, from religion to nature, family matters to politics, with both of us pressing our point of view vigorously and not giving an inch. This is another part of Annette's character that I miss so much. She was a really strong woman with strongly held views on all kinds of subjects and I loved arguing my point with her. Although we disagreed about a lot of things and held different views, particularly on religion, we respected each other's point of view. (Annette is interjecting with a thought intrusion here to say it did not seem like that at times.) We always finished our discussion or argument on a light note and never with any bitterness.

Apart from sleeping alone in an empty bed, these are the things I miss so much now. Like breakfast time, the evening meal was always such a happy time as well.When Annette came in every evening she would be so anxious to tell me about her day and the things she was doing in the council. She took such pride in her job, and always wanted to do the best she possibly could for all the groups she worked with.

Now mealtime means nothing. It only serves to remind me of what I once had and have lost. Now I just eat something when I feel like it, and a lot of the time I don't feel like it at all.

After we came back from Bulgaria in the summer of 2007 we only went to Dingle on two weekends. As Annette was now working full-time we could not spend as much time down there as we would have liked. When we did go it was always great to have the time alone and do the things we liked to do, even if only for a few days.

Life went along quite normally that year, we visited the children and occasionally baby sat for Gina. Annette was happy in her work and I was happy to be at home cooking and writing. Life could not have been more normal.

Around this time I was also trying to get my show, *Nighthawks The Musical*, up and running. Together with a few friends, Alan Fitzpatrick and Tom Quinn, we were planning a production early in 2008, but difficulties arose so it did not happen until near the end of the year. Christmas 2007 was to be the last Christmas we were all together as a family.

Early in the New Year Robert and Fiona's marriage began to unravel and they separated before the year was out. I'm not going to speak about that, as that's their story, but I will say that the hurt Robert went through caused Annette and I a lot of pain, particularly Annette as she was much more in tune with Robert's feelings than I was. She was also very fond of Fiona and regretted losing her as a family member and friend.

As Robert and Fiona's marriage was breaking up after five years, myself and Annette were getting ready to celebrate forty years together since we had first said "I do," back in 1968. It was a cause of sadness to us that it coincided with Robert and Fiona's break-up. But there was nothing we could do about that as they did not want to be reconciled. We knew from our own experience that for difficulties to be overcome both parties must want that to happen, this was not the situation with Robert and Fiona.

For our anniversary we went on a cruise to Alaska. Annette knew that I had always wanted to see Alaska since reading James Michener's novel of the same name many years before and she was happy to fall in with my plans for our anniversary when I suggested that's where we should go. We flew from Dublin to Amsterdam on Saturday, the 16th of May and from Amsterdam to San Francisco to catch our cruise ship for what turned out to be a fantastic holiday. We booked an ocean view cabin and it was a dreamlike experience to make love moving to the rhythm of the waves as the sea whished by the window.

We stayed in San Francisco for two days before boarding the ship *The Millennium* for our voyage through the Inside Passage from Vancouver to Alaska. San Francisco was a great experience. We stayed in the Hilton Hotel near Union Square, right in the heart of the city. Although we were only there for two days we managed to see a lot of the city, cross the Golden Gate Bridge, ride on the little cable cars that climb half way to the stars and dine on Fisherman's Wharf.

From Frisco we sailed to Astoria in Oregon and on to Seattle, before entering the Inside Passage from Vancouver. We visited Ketchikan, Juneau and Skagway. While in Skagway we travelled on the White Pass and Yukon railway deep into the Rockies.

Alaska was to be our last big holiday together. We had now both got to see the places we had wanted to visit for a long time, Annette had seen Brazil and visited the Favelas as well as other parts of South America and I had got to see Alaska, which turned out to be not quite the Alaska depicted by James Michner, but well worth the journey nevertheless.

Our journey together, which had started on Bray Head in 1965, was nearing its end, although we did not know it then as we enjoyed the luxury of the cruise and the Captain's formal dinners at which Annette looked so beautiful, even more beautiful than she had been when I first met her over forty years before. She had matured into a stunningly beautiful and sensual woman who I was so proud to call my wife and walk into the ballroom of the cruise ship with arm-in-arm. She looked so young and healthy and showed no signs nor had any symptoms of the changes that we now know were happening inside her body. We had a picture taken at one dinner on the cruise that now adorns Annette's head stone. Looking at that picture now it's hard to imagine how someone who looked so beautiful and healthy then could be dead ten months later.

Our Alaskan holiday was to celebrate our fortieth wedding anniversary, but when we came home we had a family celebration on the actual day, the 24th of September. The family took us out and treated us to a meal at the Avon Ri restaurant in Blessington. Annette loved family get-togethers, especially when the grandchildren were there. In the photographs taken that day you can see how happy Annette is as she holds the children. We really enjoyed that day with the family, little knowing it was to be the last anniversary we would share.

When we came back from the cruise in early June I immediately got working on *Nighthawks* which was to open in the Plaza Hotel in September. It was full speed ahead. We assembled a cast and hired a director and set about working towards an opening in September.

I did not know it then but what happened on the last night of the show was to play a crucial part in what was to transpire around Annette's passing and the events after it, events which are, even as I write this, still unfolding. I am coming to the most fantastic part of this story, and I will be totally honest here and state if anyone had told me what I'm about to tell you a year ago, I would not have believed them. But I know what happened on the last night of *Nighthawks* is true and I'm well aware of what followed. There is just one more thing I will say about that night before I get on with the story, and it's this, I'm very glad now I told people on the night what had been said to me, as it is proof that it did happen. If I had not said anything until events had unfolded I could now be accused of making it up. But it's my misfortune that what was said and what happened that night had consequences for our lives.

The events of that night and the subsequent events have caused me to change my views and beliefs on very fundamental aspects of how I now look at life and death.

Nighthawks opened in the Plaza Hotel Tallaght on Thursday, 4th September and ran that weekend and the following weekend 12th, 13th and 14th September. We brought it back for one more weekend, from 31st October – 2nd November.

Annette helped us out each night by manning the door and selling and collecting tickets. I was helping out on the sound desk so I usually left the house about an hour before Annette. On the last night, 2nd November , I went down to the Plaza before Annette as usual. When Annette arrived we spoke for a few minutes and she said to me:

"You'll never guess what happened before I left the house."

"What?" says I.

"While I was upstairs getting ready I heard a crash downstairs and when I went down our picture and your mother's memorial card were on the ground and there was a big crack in our picture, right down the middle. We must be going to separate" she laughed.

"How did they fall?" I asked.

"I don't know; I just heard a crash and they were on the floor when I went down."

"And the glass is broken?" I said.

"Yes, right down the middle" she replied.

We were interrupted after that as preparations were being made for the show and said no more about the incident. The show went on and it went down very well.

As it was the last night most people stayed back afterwards for a drink. I was sitting at a table with about seven or eight people including Annette, the hotel manager Karl Walker, his parents and a cast member Shirley Whelan. I was talking to Shirley, who was sitting facing me. Annette was sitting beside me talking to Karl's parents who were sitting to her right. After a while Shirley left to speak to someone else. I was sitting facing an empty chair when a lady whom I never saw before in my life sat down. She proceeded to make small talk for a while, saying how much she liked the show and such like. Then she said I'd have great success with it and I'd be on *The Late Late Show*. I laughed and said something like, that's hardly likely as the show had ended its run. She then said no, I'd be on *The Late Late Show* not for *Nighthawks* but for a book I would write, a book about the past. Again I laughed and tried to pass it off by making some comment or other.

The lady's demeanour then changed and she asked if I knew anyone named Mary. I laughed and said: "Everyone knows someone named Mary." She then said: "She is saying there's something about a throat." When she said this I looked at her and said: "My mother's name was Mary, she died of throat cancer and today is her anniversary." The lady said: "Yes I know, and she is here with you, she says she is looking after you, that she has helped you before and will do so again." I must have looked somewhat puzzled by this as the lady then said: "I'm a medium and I have no control over this, I was directed to you."

I then said something like, "What do you mean my mother is here?"

She replied, "She is here with you now. She says she has taken you out of tight spots before and she will do so again." She then spoke about how she'd had this power since she was much younger and had no control over what information came through her. She went on to say "Your mother is now standing behind you and she is holding up a watch. Does a watch mean anything to you, did your mother ever give you a watch or you give one to her?" I replied, "No, as far as I remember my mother never wore a watch in her life." She then said a few more things about being a medium and how she was sometimes directed towards people she did not know, people that someone on the other side wanted to contact or give a message to. There was a bit more conversation and then she asked, "Are you a gardener?" "No" I replied, "not at all, why?" She said, "Because your mother is now holding a rose over you and she is plucking the thorns from the rose." I told her this did not mean anything to me. "I think it might have a meaning you're not aware of" she said and continued, " If anyone gives you a rose, it will not be from the person giving it to you, it will be from your mother." At that point someone called me and I turned away for a moment or two. When I turned back she was gone. I looked around the room but I could not see her anywhere. She seemed to have vanished.

I sat alone for a while and then people started to leave and I turned to Annette who had just said good night to the people she had been talking to. I told her what had just transpired with the lady who was now nowhere to be seen. Annette said she had not noticed her as she was talking and was unaware who I was talking to. I reminded Annette what had happened earlier on, our picture falling, and it being my mother's anniversary, but she just laughed and said not to take it too seriously or something like that. She was not perturbed in the least by it. I thought it was most peculiar and mentioned the incident, including the picture falling, to a few people who laughingly asked if anyone had given me a rose. I put the incident out of my mind and joined in the after-show sing song.

When we got home later that night I saw the picture which had fallen off the bookshelf. It was a picture of myself and Annette which had been taken in Italy a few years before. It was cracked from the top of the frame to the bottom, separating us completely. From the large crack ran a smaller crack, right across my heart. I thought little more about this incident until after Christmas when Annette was diagnosed with throat cancer. Then I tried to find out the identity of the lady who had approached me that night.

Annette hard at work cleaning chalets in Le Littoral

Annette carrying the cross on the Via Dolorosa in Jerusalem

Our second "marriage" in Cana of Galilee October 2000

Report of our trip to Israel

Annette takes a nap in a hammock in Brazil

At Iguazu Falls

At the statue of Christ the Redeemer Rio de Janeiro

Alaska 2008

The last night of "Nighthawks" Annette with Shirley Whelan and Peter Morrissey

With our grandchildren, Senan, Ella-May and Mina

Annette with Mina

Annette with Senan and Ella-May at the spot we first met in 1965 on Bray Head

The last picture of Annette taken two weeks before she passed away

REMEMBERING ANNETTE

On the 27th March the tribute concert **Remembering Annette** took place in the Civic Theatre, Tallaght. Annette Halpin was well known to many in the Traveller community, especially for her social inclusion & development work with Traveller women's groups in areas such as Tallaght and Leixleip. After a brave battle with cancer Annette's journey in this world came to an end on 14th April 2009.

At the request of her husband, Andy and the family I was very privileged to celebrate Annette's Funeral Mass. Later on, at the time of her Month's Mind Mass, in speaking with Andy about Annette I heard about their musical setting of the life of Saint Patrick. So when Andy contacted me some months ago to take the part of narrator, I was very happy to agree. I was glad to be associated with Annette & Andy's creative work, glad to have a part in highlighting the very relevant story of Saint Patrick particularly in this the **Year of Evangelisation**, and also glad as parish priest in the Parish of the Travelling People to have been able to build on the close relationship Annette had with Travellers in her work and through her music.

Knowing Annette from my time in St. Martin's Parish, and as a fellow pilgrim in Medjugorje, soon after my arrival in the Parish of the Travelling People, Annette

invited me to come to meet the Leixleip Traveller Women's Group she was then working with. In the context of that work it was particularly special that members of the **Traveller Parish Choir**, formed especially for the event were a part of the tribute to Annette, and also took the lead in performing her song **'Everyone'**.

I know that Annette was greatly saddened at tragic death of one of the young women in the Leixleip group, Ellen Lawrence, just shortly before her own death. Around this time of their First Anniversaries, we remember them both in the old prayer: 'Light of Heaven to them, may they rest in peace'.

Fr. Derek

Article published in The Traveller Magazine

Chapter Twenty Five

A nnette developed a sore throat in July after we came back from Alaska, nothing serious, just a normal sore throat that most people get from time to time. She went to the doctor who examined her and prescribed antibiotics. After she'd finished the medicine the sore throat persisted so she went back to the doctor. Annette was given more antibiotics and sent for an X-ray in Tallaght Hospital at the end of July. The X-ray did not show anything unusual and Annette continued working. She thought the sore throat would go in time as at one point it did seem to be less sore than it had been.

During all this time Annette seemed quite healthy apart from the nagging sore throat. In August we went to Dingle with Gina, Senan and Ella for a few days and Annette was fine. We also went to Spain for a week at the end of September, where we met up with Ciara's parents, Martin and Marie Byrne. They were friends of Annette's long before David and Ciara ever met. It was while we were in Spain that Annette first displayed a slight discomfort in eating, but nothing serious, she could still eat her meals.

When we came back from Spain Annette went back to the doctor, who examined her again. He found nothing out of the ordinary and prescribed another course of antibiotics which failed to clear the sore throat. She also had another X-ray, this time at the Charlemount Clinic. Again nothing unusual showed up.

Towards the end of November Annette began to have a bit more difficulty in swallowing her food but she was still able to eat a full meal. She still felt well and was continuing to work and do all the things she normally did. I asked her once or twice to go back to the doctor, but she said there was no point as she'd had two X-rays, taken the antibiotics and it would probably go in time.

Annette did not feel sick and we went for a weekend break to Wexford in early December. As far as I can remember she was able to eat her meals but at a somewhat slower pace. But coming up to Christmas things suddenly got worse with regard to her swallowing ability.

On the Tuesday of Christmas week I persuaded Annette to go to the Eye and Ear hospital on Adelaide Road. We got to the "emergency" department at 5.10 p.m. to be told, with some glee by the receptionist that they did not see "throats" or "ears" after five, only "eyes", and they would not be open again till after Christmas.

We left the hospital and headed down Grafton Street. We took in the Christmas atmosphere and had what turned out to be our last restaurant meal together in Bewleys, two bowls of soup, beef for me vegetable for Annette. Despite her inability to eat solids Annette was in good form and did not feel unwell. In our ignorance of how cancer operates this probably led us to a false sense that nothing too serious was wrong with her.

We went to Gina's for Christmas dinner, which for Annette was mashed potato and jelly for afters. The danger signals were now flashing brightly.

Annette went back to the doctor the day after Stephen's Day. After examining her he wanted her to go to Tallaght Hospital for an MRI-scan. At this point we wanted to find out what Annette's problem was without further delay so we opted to go to the Beacon Clinic and have the scan done there instead of waiting around Tallaght for days.

Myself, Annette and Robert went to the Beacon Clinic at two o'clock on Monday, 29th December, 2008, the day our world was turned upside down and control of our lives was taken from us. The day we became like dead fish floating in a river not knowing what was happening to us.

Annette was treated with full professionalism by the doctors in the Beacon, but when we presented ourselves at the reception desk all the receptionist seemed to be interested in was if we could afford to be there. We were never asked what was wrong, who was the patient, were they in pain, or did we want a glass of water. We were shown a "menu" with prices and asked how we wished to pay for whatever it was we wanted. I really felt that if I had queried anything on the price list security would have been called and we would have been thrown out. What an introduction to a "caring" institution. But as I have said, once passed the reception Annette was treated without delay and with all due care.

After the scan was taken we were asked to wait for the result and were given a cup of tea. We did not have to wait long. When the doctor came back with the result of the scan his words were the beginning of our lives being shattered. He said the scan had shown up something, possibly a tumour, maybe cancerous, but more tests would have to be carried out to ascertain that.

At the mention of the word cancerous Annette and I looked at each other in shock and disbelief. At no time since Annette had developed her sore throat had we ever thought of it being cancer. Cancer was just not on the radar. She was not sick, or at that time losing weight, cancer was just not possible. I thought people with cancer were very sick and in pain, with the weight falling off them. Annette did not fit into that category at all.

I held Annette's hand as the doctor continued. He said he was going to make arrangements for Annette to go to St. James's hospital for further tests as they did not have the necessary facilities in the Beacon. When Annette asked when this would be, he replied "straight away". He felt that it was important that she should begin getting treatment as soon as possible as the tumour was quite large.

I asked if we would have to go to the A & E and wait half the night before being seen, but he said no, he would contact a Dr. O'Neill right away. He told us to go to the triage nurse and we would be seen without delay.

In a state of shock we thanked him and went back to the waiting area. We told Robert we had to go to St. James's immediately. I don't know if we mentioned cancer to him at that point, we possibly only said at that time that his Mam had to have more tests carried out. We paid the bill at 'Checkpoint Charlie' and headed for St. James's hospital without delay.

When we reached St. James's we went straight to the triage nurse's office as instructed. She was expecting us and took us through to an area at the back of the A & E Department where we were told Dr. O'Neill would be with us as soon as possible. He had been called to Tallaght Hospital so we had to wait until he came back. After about an hour Dr. O'Neill arrived. He was a tall, youngish man with a very nice manner.

He obviously had the report from the Beacon Clinic, so he spoke to Annette about what he was going to do. He had to put a camera down the back of her throat, through her nose to look at whatever was there. He did this with the minimum of discomfort to Annette and what he saw was serious. Dr. O'Neill confirmed that there was a large tumour in her throat but he could not at this point say whether it was cancerous or not. Further tests and a biopsy would have to be carried out.

He said he wanted Annette to stay in St. James's that night as he was anxious that she get a bed and be in the hospital when full services were resumed after the New Year. This was a further shock to us as we had not at all expected Annette to have to stay in overnight but Dr. O'Neill was insistent that this was the best course of action. With the New Year coming up in a day or two, if Annette waited any longer to secure a bed she might not get one. He said that she could go home the next day and come back that night as he only wanted her to have a bed to be sure she would get treated as soon as possible.

This was an entirely unexpected development that we just were not prepared for. Annette protested that she had no clothes with her but Dr O'Neill said that was not a problem as the hospital would supply her with a night dress and she could go home the next day and bring back whatever she needed.

I knew at this point that things were serious, so I said to Annette that I thought she should do as the doctor wanted. I promised I would collect her the following morning and bring her home and she could pick up any clothes she needed. Dr O'Neill said she could do this for the next few days, go home each day but be back in the hospital by nine o'clock at night until after the new year when she would have to stay in and have the tests done.

Reluctantly Annette agreed to this. Dr O'Neill then said he would make arrangements for Annette to have a bed as soon as possible. He told us to wait in the area behind the A & E and when a bed was ready Annette would be called. This was at about nine or nine thirty.

By eleven o'clock that night Annette was in a bed in St. John's Ward. Myself and Robert stayed with Annette for a while. When the nurse brought her the night clothes we had to say our goodbyes. I slept alone that night, the start of what was to become long, lonely nights in the big, empty bed.

The next day I told Gina and David what had happened in the Beacon. I then went in on the Luas to collect Annette and bring her home. At that point we did not know how serious this would turn out to be. Although cancer had been mentioned, we were not convinced or prepared to believe that Annette actually had cancer, cancer happened to other people, not to us. Anyway, Annette looked too well to have cancer, she wasn't sick. The tests would show the doctors' suspicions were wrong. It was probably only an abscess or something like that. These were the thoughts I was arming myself with as I refused to face the possibility that there was something serious wrong with Annette.

When Annette came home the next day she packed a bag with night clothes and other stuff for what she was hoping would be a short stay in St. James's. We then had some soup and headed into town to meet Gina. We were taking Senan and Ella to the pantomime in the Olympia. That's how 'sick' Annette felt, she was still doing all the ordinary things expected of a nana at Christmas time. It was what was giving us hope that the doctors were wrong about a cancerous tumour causing her swallowing problems.

After the show, Gina collected the children from us at the Olympia and we all went to the film centre. We had coffee and soup, with ice cream for the children before Annette and I headed back to the hospital for 9 p.m. I stayed with Annette until after 11 p.m. when I left to get the Luas home, feeling good that Annette felt and looked so well.

The next day was New Years Eve, always a big day for Annette and me. We always had some kind of a celebration on New Years Eve. The year before we had gone to a favourite restaurant of ours, Tante Zoe's in Temple Bar. We'd had a meal and then met Annette's sisters in the Sheldon Hotel where we celebrated until about two o'clock in the morning. As things turned out that was to be the last time we would celebrate a New Year's Eve together.

I went to St. James's early on Wednesday morning to collect Annette. We went to the Square in Tallaght as Annette wanted to get some things for her stay in hospital. She met some friends in the Square who were very surprised when she told them of the recent developments. They commented on how well she looked.

We went home and I made Annette some soup which she was able to drink. We had a snooze for a while in the afternoon before Robert came down to bring us back to the hospital that evening. Before going to the hospital we had a glass of wine to celebrate the New Year. This was also the first time we talked about what was happening. Up to this point we had avoided any serious talk, and although cancer had been mentioned we avoided talking about it. Even then when Annette asked me what I thought was going to happen I assured her that she would be fine. I said that I did not believe it was cancer as she did not look like someone who had a serious illness and she was not losing weight. I tried to convince her (and myself) that everything was going to be alright. I took her in my arms, and as I held her we both shed a few tears.

Robert and I stayed with Annette until about eleven o'clock on New Years Eve. I kissed her and wished her a Happy New Year, telling her that normal service would be resumed next year.

Robert stayed with me that night and we had a few bottles of beer in the house. At midnight we went out onto the green and wished some neighbours a Happy New Year. When they asked about Annette I just said she had to go into hospital for some tests and she should be out in a couple of days.

We kept up the routine of Annette spending the days at home and going back to the hospital every night until Sunday, when she would go in for good. I went in on the Luas to collect her on Sunday morning, but since the day was very bad, cold and raining, we got a taxi home. We stopped at a shop in Springfield to pick up a few fire logs and a small bag of coal. I lit the fire and made soup for Annette and we had it in front of the fire. It was a miserable day, but the fire was cheerful. After we had the soup we sat on the couch and began to snooze.

After a while Annette asked me if I would I like to go up to bed. She said this might be the last chance we would have for a while to make love. While I always wanted to make love to Annette I was conscious of the fact that she was sick. I did not want to be selfish or make her feel she had to do it just because she was going into hospital for a while. I told Annette this, but she said she would like to, and she felt fine. We put the fireguard in front of the fire, locked the door, went up to bed and made love for the last time.

CHAPTER TWENTY SIX

Later that evening Robert drove us to the hospital and Annette started what was to be the final stage of her own journey in this life. When the hospital got back to full service the next day the doctors visited Annette and made arrangements for her to have more tests and a biopsy.

On the morning of the biopsy I went down later than usual as I knew she would be in the theatre. By this time Annette had been shifted to Private Two in St. James's and she had a room of her own. When I looked into the room at about twelve o'clock it was empty. I went to the nurses' station and asked about Annette. The nurse told me she had had to have a tracheostomy and would be back later as she was in recovery. I just said, "Oh did she." I didn't have a clue at that point what a tracheostomy was, as no one had mentioned it to us or the fact that Annette might need one.

I went for a walk and came back an hour or so later. Annette was back in her room. When I saw her I was shocked. She was still groggy after her operation, but what was shocking was the sight of the tube sticking out of her throat. She was very tired so I only stayed a while but before I left I asked the nurse about the tube in her throat. I was told it was to help her breathe. But as she'd never had any difficulty breathing I did not understand this explanation. The nurse told me that the doctors would be around later and they would speak to me about it.

I honestly can't remember what I did then but later that evening I went back to the hospital. While I was sitting in the room with Annette, who was sleeping and who could not talk because of the tracheostomy, a Dr. Tynan and his team came around.

Now Dr. Tynan was not Annette's doctor. She had, as I understood it, been under the care of Dr. Kinsella, whom we had spoken to. He had told us about the biopsy but had not mentioned anything about a tracheostomy nor indeed about Annette's breathing being a problem.

Dr. Tynan called me out of the room and I asked him about the tube in Annette's throat. He said that he had had to perform a tracheostomy because he believed that had he not done so Annette would have gone into respiratory arrest in a few days. There was a danger he believed that her air tube would close, at which point an emergency tracheotomy would have been necessary. I tried to say that there was nothing wrong with her breathing yesterday and that Dr. Kinsella had not said anything to us about a tracheotomy being necessary, but he continued talking, he said that Annette had a very large tumour in her throat which he believed would have impinged on her air tube and prevented her breathing in a very short time. He continued, saying it was inoperable and nothing could be done for her. He said they could not cure her.

I stood listening to this in a daze. I heard the words he was saying but I was trying not to. I felt like putting my hands over my ears and running away. He was speaking in a not very sympathetic and matter-of-fact way. I broke down and started to cry.

One of his team tried to console me as Dr. Tynan continued talking. He asked if I had a family, and when I said I had, he said I should inform them straight away. I said I would tell them tomorrow, as it was now after nine o'clock, but he said, no, tell them tonight.

I was now in a state of shock. I thought Annette would not last the night. I think at this point Dr. Tynan said he was sorry to have to give me such bad news but there was nothing they could do for Annette, the tumour was too large and it may have spread. Again he told me to go home and tell the family. He said that Annette would be alright that night.

Dr. Tynan and his team then left me with the ward nurses who offered me a cup of tea. I refused the tea and went back into Annette's room. She was still sleeping so I kissed her and sat with her for a few minutes. After being assured by the nurses that she would be alright that night, I went home.

I think I cried all the way home in the Luas as I tried to come to terms with what I had been told. Suddenly everything had changed. From the optimism of a few days ago I was now faced with the total devastation of all hope. Annette was going to die, and nothing could be done about it. I did not know what to do about telling the family. Should I tell them tonight or wait until tomorrow? But that decision was made for me.

As I was walking home crying after getting off the Luas, my mobile rang. It was Annette's brother Liam. I answered, choking with tears. When he asked about Annette I just blurted it all out. Liam asked where I was and I told him I was on my way home. He asked if there was anyone with me and I said no, so Liam insisted on coming over to be with me.

As I turned the corner to our house I saw Robert's car outside the door. I went in, and still crying told Robert the awful news. I could do nothing but sit on the couch and cry. I told Robert that Liam was on his way over. Robert then rang Gina and David and told them, I spoke to both of them and told them that nothing would happen that night and not to come over to the house. They were both very upset at this completely unexpected turn of events. None of us had had any doubts that Annette would get better, losing her was the last thing on our minds. This was turning into a nightmare.

Liam arrived soon afterwards. He was also very upset and could not believe what was happening. We tried to rationalise it, but it just did not make sense, Annette had not been sick, she only had a sore throat and could not swallow. People did not die from a sore throat. As we were talking Gina arrived. She was very distressed and had got a taxi over from Celbridge. We went over the whole thing, again and again, but we just could not accept what we had been told.

After cups of tea and biscuits and endlessly dissecting what the doctor had said it was now very late. I told Gina to go home and we would go to the hospital tomorrow and speak to Annette's own doctor, Dr Kinsella, about what could be done. Liam said he would tell the sisters when he got home. They left but Robert insisted on staying with me that night. We were now really feeling like the dead fish in a river, we were just been carried along by events, with no control whatsoever over our final destination.

I went into the hospital the next morning and was amazed to find Annette up out of the bed. She was in the bathroom, washing herself. This was the woman who had undergone a very serious operation, and who I had been told had inoperable cancer. Now here she was looking remarkably well, standing in front of the bathroom mirror having a wash. As I kissed her the nurse came in. She said she had never seen anyone up and about the day after a tracheostomy operation. But despite looking so well Annette was upset about the tracheostomy. Like me she had not expected it, and as she indicated to me that she could not talk, tears filled her eyes. She came out of the bathroom and got back into bed.

I didn't know what to say to her as I was totally in the dark about the trachie myself, and had not yet spoken to Dr. Kinsella. The only way we could now communicate was by me talking and Annette writing her replies in a copy book. She asked me about the tracheostomy and why she had to have it. I told her what Dr Tynan had told me about his fear that her air tube was about to close.

Annette wrote, "Orla (a member of Dr. Kinsella's team) examined me the night before and said my airway was open. I need my voice, I was not expecting this. Tynan is supposed to be very good, maybe when they looked inside it was different. Did he say anything else?"

I did not tell her the rest of what he had said. I told her that I hoped to see Dr Kinsella later and maybe he would be able to tell us more. Another effect of the trachie was that Annette could not eat or drink through her mouth. They had fitted a peg in her stomach through which food and water would be given to her. It was also impossible for her to lie flat on her back or on her side. She had to sit upright in the bed so she could breathe through the tube in her neck. In the space of one day a huge emotional burden had been inflicted on Annette, a woman who loved to talk and sing was now rendered speechless, though not voiceless. She used the note pad to express her needs and views as strongly as ever.

Later when she was given a plastic voice box, she did her best to master it. It was great to hear sounds coming from her mouth again. As soon as Annette was recovered sufficiently from her operation she went around the other wards in Private Two, blessing people with a Padre Pio relic a friend had sent her. Despite her own difficulties she was still concerned about others.

This is not an easy time to recall or write about. Indeed a lot of what happened immediately after Annette had her trachie operation is very hazy now. It was an appalling time for all the family, to see a once vibrant and loving person reduced to a shell of her former self and unable to speak. In truth, I can't distinguish one day from another during this period. I went to the hospital every morning, staying until nine or ten every night. Then I went home to a cold, empty house in the worst winter I can ever remember. The snow seemed to never be going to thaw. For weeks on end, I trudged home from the Luas through the ice. I had a quick cup of coffee and something to eat and went to bed in a back bedroom, amid the dust and rubble of a building site. During this time we were getting the two front bedrooms converted into one. We had been told that when Annette did come home we would need room for all her feeding equipment and medication and also just to give her more space and comfort. We had moved into a front bedroom from the big back bedroom many years before when all the children were at home. We had divided the large bedroom so that they would have a bedroom each. We had always intended to reconvert the back bedroom or to enlarge the front bedroom over the years, but we had always spent the money on travel or some other luxury and continued to sleep in the small front room. It was no hardship to do this as the front room was cosy, with a view of the mountains and very conducive to intimacy. We spent many happy years in that little room and filled it with love. I sleep in the "new" big bedroom alone now, but I just cannot feel it was ever "our" bedroom.

When I did speak to Dr. Kinsella a day or so later he was more positive than Dr. Tynan had been, and felt it was possible to operate. He said all the scans taken so far indicated that the cancer was confined to the throat and had not spread elsewhere. This was a bit of good news amid all the despondency we now felt. He also said the chances of complete success were very slim because of the size of the cancer, but he felt it was possible that he could prolong Annette's life. He said that as long as the cancer had not spread he would operate on Annette to remove the tumour from her throat. To be sure this was the case he said he would make arrangements for Annette to have a "PET scan in Blackrock Clinic. If this was clear he would operate as soon as Annette had recovered from the trachie operation which he assured us had been necessary.

During this time Annette was visited by other medical people and members of Dr. Kinsella's team. Arrangements were made by the speech therapist for a lady who had had a similar operation fifteen years previously to come in and talk to Annette about what to expect after it. We were all very encouraged by this lady's visit. She was able to speak quite well with the aid of a stoma in her throat. She was leading a perfectly normal life, including working in a job where she had to use her voice. Annette took great heart from the visit, and provided the PET scan was clear, felt she could cope just as well after her operation.

A few days later Annette went to Blackrock Clinic for her scan. For two days we all held our breath as we awaited the result which we hoped would allow her to have the operation. As soon as the doctors told her the good news, that the cancer was confined to her throat, she sent me a text. I'm writing it down exactly as I got it, 'docors around pet scan clear surgery for tuesday love xx'

I later spoke to Dr. Kinsella who said the scan had confirmed that the cancer was localised in the throat and that subject to a bed being available in the intensive care unit the operation was to go ahead on Tuesday, 20th January.

I continued to visit Annette each day and we were very positive that the operation would be a success. Apart from the difficulty she had talking, Annette was feeling fine. She had recovered well from the trachie operation and was up and about. She loved going for a walk around the hospital. When the grandchildren were brought in she was always concerned about them visiting the ward as she was afraid they might contract something so she always insisted on meeting them in the cafe. She loved to see Senan, Ella and Mina, but she was sad that Senan, who was four, seemed to be afraid of her new voice and appearance. The two girls, who were only two years old, were less aware of the difference in Annette and did not react in the same way.

As the day set for the operation drew near, Annette was visited by the various teams of doctors who would be assisting Dr. Kinsella and each of them explained the part they would play in the operation. All this attention was very encouraging. They all seemed to believe that everything would go as planned and Annette would soon be rid of the cancer. We knew that even if the operation was a success, it would still be a long time before Annette would be back to anything like she was before all this had started. But talking to the various teams of doctors and seeing the confidence they displayed, in turn gave us confidence that things would turn out right.

The night before the operation we still did not know if the intensive care bed would be available. We were told they would only know that on the morning of the operation, but that everything was going ahead on the assumption that a bed would be available.

On the morning of the 20th I was in the hospital by eight o'clock. I sat with Annette until we got word, at about ten o'clock, that a bed was confirmed and the operation was going ahead. It was then all systems go as Annette was prepared for surgery. She was very composed and did not seem to be in the least worried about what was ahead of her. As usual, she had her rosary beads with her and her Miraculous medal was pinned to her gown.

I went down to the operating theatre with her and stayed with her until the anaesthetist came and took her into the theatre. This was around 11.30 a.m. I can remember it clearly. I kissed her as she was sitting up on the gurney. She was smiling and waving to me as she was taken through the doors of the theatre. I waited until she was gone from view and then left.

I got the Luas home to wait the seven or eight hours we had been told the operation would take. On the way I rang the family to let them know the operation was underway. That was the start of a very anxious day.

After I got home I listened to the radio for a while. It was Inauguration Day in America so there was plenty to listen to. It was good to be distracted from the thoughts that were in my mind. Later that day Gina and Robert came over. We were all looking at the Inauguration on the TV at about 5.45 p.m. when the phone rang. It was the hospital. They wanted us to come down as soon as possible. The person on the phone would not give us any information about Annette, just asked us to come down as soon as we could.

I knew at once this was not going to be good news. We went straight away. When we reached the hospital we went directly up to Private Two. We were met by a nurse who brought us to a waiting room and told us Dr. Kinsella would be with us soon. We did not say very much to each other. We were all caught up in our own thoughts and afraid to express them.

After a few minutes Dr. Kinsella arrived and the expression on his face said it all. I thought Annette had died during the operation. He sat down and seemed to be gathering his thoughts, working out what he was going to say to us.

We remained silent and waited for him to speak. "I'm afraid it's not good news," he said.

There was an audible gasp and I immediately asked, "Is she dead?" Dr. Kinsella replied, "No, she's still in the theatre, but I'm afraid the operation was not a success." He then went on to explain that five hours into the operation he had discovered that the cancer was in the oesophagus. There was no way of operating there. He had removed some of the tumour in her neck but he said he could not cure Annette. The operation had to be abandoned. Annette was being moved to the intensive care unit and we could see her there later.

After more talk and discussion I asked Dr. Kinsella how much time Annette had left. He said he would be surprised if she was alive by Christmas.

This was shocking news for us. Despite all we had been told we had never contemplated Annette dying. We just did not think of it at all. I for one had been convinced that Annette would beat the cancer. She had not seemed sick at all. Even going into the operating theatre she had been sitting up and smiling, with seemingly not a care in the world. Hearing what Dr. Kinsella had just said was shattering news.

The doctor tried to console us by saying that everything possible would be done for Annette. He toned down his assessment that Annette would be dead by Christmas, saying that was only his opinion and he had been wrong in the past. Someone, I don't know who, phoned David with the bad news.

After Dr. Kinsella left we made our way to the intensive care unit and waited to be allowed to see her. When we were admitted into the ward we were completely unprepared for the condition she was in. I knew Annette had to be cut in the neck but I was appalled when I saw the extent of the wound. She had been cut from ear to ear, as if her neck had been slashed open. A semi-circle of staple like stitches was visible, like a necklace around her neck.

Annette was unconscious, still under the effect of the anaesthetic. She was not aware we were there. We stayed for a while and then spoke to a nurse who told us she would be like that for the rest of the night.

I honestly do not remember going home that night but I know we did.

Chapter Twenty Seven

The next few days are just a haze. I do not remember much about them at all. I remember being with Annette after she was released from Intensive Care into the High Dependency Unit. At this point she was fully conscious but she did not know that the operation had been unsuccessful.

She was released from High Dependency after a day and was back in Private Two. She continued to make a rapid recovery from the operation. The family spoke about the situation, and what we should do about telling Annette that the operation had not removed all the cancer. We had a meeting with Dr. Kinsella where he explained that Annette, as a fully comprehending adult was entitled to know the truth about the operation and he was obliged to tell her. After a very helpful discussion Dr. Kinsella said that he believed Annette would benefit from radiotherapy and chemotherapy and, while he did not believe this treatment would cure the cancer, it could prolong her life. This treatment would be carried out at St. Luke's Hospital. Dr. Kinsella said he would speak to his colleagues about this course of action.

Annette seemed to be getting stronger all the time and it was hard to take on board what Dr. Kinsella was telling us. She was coping very well with the situation though she was finding it hard to sleep in an upright position. We somehow managed not to mention how the operation had gone and I continually told her she was going to get better.

We had agreed at the meeting that we would accompany Dr. Kinsella when he told Annette about the operation. He also agreed with my suggestion that he would not mention the word "terminal" or say anything about the length of time Annette had left. The day Dr. Kinsella was to tell Annette the operation had failed was finally upon us and we were dreading it.

I did not know how Annette would react to this awful news as I had never stopped telling her how much I believed she was getting better. Whether this was the right thing to do or not

I just did not know. I wanted to boost her spirits and not be moping around her with a glum face. Maybe I believed that if Annette saw how confident we were she would get better again, that this belief would actually make her better. In the situation we were in you tend to grasp at anything.

I had arranged to meet Gina, David and Robert at the hospital cafe on the day we were due to meet Dr. Kinsella. When Dr. Kinsella was ready, we would all go with him to see Annette. We were waiting for him in the cafe but as he approached our table he did not look happy. He sat down and said there had been a hitch in the plans. Prof. Hollywood who was attached to St. Luke's Hospital had, unknown to Dr. Kinsella, visited Annette that morning. He had told her about the operation and the plans to treat her in St. Luke's. To say that we were annoyed is putting it mildly. We had wanted to be with Annette when she was told this news so we could support and console her. We also did not know just what or how much Prof. Hollywood had told Annette. Everyone, including the nurses on the ward, was very annoyed by this development.

When we went to see Annette we did not know what to expect or what her reaction to the news would be. We entered Annette's room in trepidation but she was as composed as could be, sitting up in the bed smiling and looking great.

I said, "I heard Prof. Hollywood has been to see you."

Annette, "Yes he told me about the operation not being a success, they did not get all the cancer."

Me, "But they are going to send you to St. Luke's for more treatment and they'll get it there."

Annette, "I don't know if I'll be able for that."

Me, "Of course you will. Look at how quickly you've recovered from that major operation and the scar on your neck is healing very quickly as well. You'll be fine, you're going to beat this."

We told Annette that we had hoped to tell her ourselves and we did not know that Prof. Hollywood was going to see her. Annette did not seem to be upset about the news. She said that he had explained that the tumour was much bigger than they'd thought and it had spread to her oesophagus. He'd told her it was not possible to operate there. She seemed to know everything Dr. Kinsella was going to tell her. But we did not know if she knew that the cancer was incurable and terminal and we were afraid to ask.

Annette made great progress from the operation and most of the time was in good form. From time to time, but not very often she did get a bit down and asked how she had got this cancer. I never said anything to her about what Dr. Kinsella had told us about the cancer being incurable and that he did not expect her to live until Christmas. I was always positive and continually told Annette she was going to get better. I wanted this to be true and for her to remain optimistic. I wanted her to see that we were positive about her recovering as well.

It was very distressing to see her struggling to speak. For Annette this must have been a very frightening experience as she loved to talk and express her opinions. She used a copy book to write her questions and answers to us and her visitors. A horrible side effect of the tracheostomy was that from time to time mucus would block the tube in her neck. This would cause Annette to have difficulty in breathing. If she could not cough the mucus up she would have to be "suctioned" by a nurse. This meant that a thin tube would be inserted into the larger tube protruding from Annette's neck and the mucus would be drawn up and out of Annette's system, with the help of a machine. This allowed her to breath normally again. It was a truly horrible procedure and one we would have to learn to do ourselves when Annette was sent home. Another cause of pain and distress was the "peg" that had been inserted into her stomach to feed her from a bottle and to give her liquids from a syringe. This was heartbreaking to see, and Annette often said how much she would love a glass of water.

In spite of all these handicaps Annette recovered well from her operation. Within a week or so she was up and walking around and we used venture to the main door of the hospital and look out at the real world beyond the hospital gates.

By St. Valentine's Day Annette was getting ready to go home. I brought her up a bouquet of balloons which said "I love you," a card and a candle holder engraved with expressions of love. It was to be our last Valentine's Day together. Annette gave me a card and a box of Roses' sweets. Arrangements had been made for her to have seven weeks of treatment in St Luke's. We were hoping it would start in early March. She had been to St. Luke's to be assessed by Prof. Hollywood and his team. She had also been fitted out with a face mask she would have to wear while having radiation treatment on her neck. There was nothing more the hospital or Dr. Kinsella could do for Annette now. Arrangements were made with the relevant people for supplies of food, syringes, a suction machine and other necessary medication to be delivered to our home in Tallaght and Annette was allowed home.

On 20th February, exactly one month after her operation, Annette was released from St. James's Hospital and she came home to her new and bigger bedroom, which had been made by taking down the partition wall and making one large room out of the two smaller rooms. Annette loved the new room with its views of the snow-covered mountains and we positioned the bed facing the windows. There was plenty of space for all the food and other equipment Annette now needed.

I cried when I saw the room being filled with all the medication. It was no longer our bedroom, the little cosy room where we had enjoyed such happy times and made passionate love so often in the past. It was now a hospital ward. Even today, so many months after those terrible events I still cannot think of it as "our" bedroom. We never made love in this room.

With Annette home, the next stage was St. Luke's and the treatment we all hoped would prolong her life. We were all anxious for the treatment to start as soon as possible. I contacted the hospital on a number of occasions to enquire when it would start. In the meantime, as I did not drive, a number of Annette's friends and some neighbours volunteered to co-operate with the family to drive Annette to St. Luke's each day. A rota was drawn up listing the days each person would be available. This was a gesture we were very grateful for. It would have been impossible to get Annette to St. Luke's and back each day without incurring great expense and a lot of inconvenience, so let me put on record again our thanks and great appreciation of the help given to us and the generosity of all concerned, Fidelma, Maureen, Wally, Jennie, Valerie, Margaret and Tony, I sincerely hope I am not forgetting anyone.

When Annette came home in February it was less than eight weeks since she had first gone into hospital. In that time our whole world and way of life had been upended. Eight weeks before Annette seemed to be a healthy, confident, vibrant woman with many years of life still ahead of her. Her only problem was a sore throat which meant she had some difficulty swallowing, which we thought was nothing very serious. Now she was a shadow of her old self. I won't say she was fearful, but she had a more nervous disposition. It was brought about not by the cancer, but by the constant fear that the trachie tube would become blocked by mucus. At this point the cancer was a lesser concern than the trachie. We did not venture out much between Annette coming home and the beginning of her treatment in March. This was principally because the weather was so cold and Annette did not want to get cold air into her tube. From time to time we did go for a short walk when it was not too cold and Robert took us out a few times for a drive. On a couple of occasions Annette drove her car around to Mass on Sunday mornings. She met her friends in the church choir and they were delighted to see how well she was doing. Her family and friends also came visiting during this time. Annette was delighted when some of her friends from her prayer group came and held prayer sessions with her. This was a great comfort to Annette. I believe she derived strength from these prayer meetings.

Annette's feeding regime meant that we had to go to bed early each night. It took twelve hours for a bottle of food to pass through the peg in Annette's stomach, and she also had to have water through a syringe. I set up the feed for Annette every night and helped her with her medication. It was just two Panadol and half a sleeping tablet. I filled and turned on the humidifier we had in the bedroom, to help prevent mucus building up in her tube. It was heartbreaking to do so and look on helplessly as the woman I loved seemed to physically diminish before my eyes. She never complained about the new way of living we were forced to endure.

I was devastated when I looked at Annette with the feeding tube hanging out of her and watched her trying to sleep while sitting upright in the bed. With these restrictions I could not even hold her close to comfort her, but I tried to get as close to her as I could without in any way dislodging the feeding tube. It was a terrible way to have to sleep. I had always held Annette close in bed and loved to snuggle and caress her body. Now we were forced to sleep at a distance.

Each morning when we woke up the first thing I did was to pull over the curtains so Annette could see the mountains which she loved. She then held my hand as she said a prayer of thanksgiving for getting through the night. As we had a little kiss and cuddle Annette would always say her little mantra, which she found so consoling and which gave her such comfort, "One day at a time, One day at a time." Holding my hand and looking into my eyes she would say, "All is well, All is well." The days of breakfast in bed served on the old silver hot-tray were over for good now. From the time Annette came out of hospital on 20th February, until her admittance to St. Luke's on Wednesday, 8th April, this was our way of life.

Annette started her chemotherapy and radiation treatment on 10th March. It was due to last seven weeks, thirty-five sessions, Monday to Friday. Radiation would be administered on each of the five days and then she would have both chemo and radiation on the Thursday of each week. Before the treatment started Prof. Hollywood told us that after about two weeks Annette would get very fatigued and it might be necessary to admit her to St Luke's as an in patient, he'd said that this was quite normal and nothing to get worried about. While Annette did feel very tired she did not get as fatigued as we had thought she would, so for four weeks she went to St. Luke's each day for her treatment.

At the end of the fourth week, on Friday, 3rd April, as was normal, she went to see the doctors from Prof. Hollywood's team for their weekly assessment. They were delighted with her condition and said they were happy for her to continue as an out-patient for a while longer, as she was not as fatigued as they had expected her to be at this stage of the treatment. This was great news for us and Annette was delighted. When I heard what the doctors said and when I saw how well Annette reacted to the news over the weekend, I was totally convinced that she would prove Dr. Kinsella wrong and survive the cancer.

Martin and Marie Byrne, Ciara's parents visited Annette on the Saturday. Marie confided to me that before coming she had been afraid of the condition Annette might be in as they had not seen her since the previous September when we were all in Spain together , Ciara had kept them informed about events and they were both amazed and delighted at how well Annette looked and sounded that weekend. She really was in great form.

On the Sunday Robert drove her to Mass in the Priory and then took us for a short drive in the country. On the way home we stopped and she walked for twenty minutes or so around Tymon Park. Things were really looking good. I believed that all the positive things I had been saying to Annette, combined with the treatment and what the doctors had said on Friday, were beginning to have the desired effect. I was sure she believed she could get through this bad period and come out the other side.

Chapter Twenty Eight

All this positivity changed the next morning as we were getting ready to go to St. Luke's. Annette was in the bathroom, washing herself, when she began to cough. She became distressed. I heard her and went in to see what was wrong. On a few previous occasions she had had difficulty dislodging mucus from the tube and I had to suction her to get it up, so at first I was not too concerned. I brought her into the bedroom and sat her on the bed. I then got the suction machine ready.

Annette was visibly upset and seemed to be in more discomfort than when we'd had to use the suction machine before. I inserted the suction tube into the tube in her neck and tried to move the mucus but nothing happened. Annette was getting more distressed. The mucus was not coming up and her face began to change colour. I got frightened and rang the ambulance service. After ringing for help I kept trying to clear the mucus. I inserted a new suction tube and finally succeeded in getting the mucus up. Annette began to feel better and she did not want the ambulance to come so I rang them again. I told them everything was alright and we did not need them. But as soon as I put the phone down Annette began to get caught again. I got to work on the suction machine again. Annette seemed to be getting worse and her colour changed.

David, who was going to drive us to the hospital that morning, then arrived. He came up to the bedroom and was shocked at what was happening. I was having no success at clearing the mucus and Annette was now turning a deep red/purple colour. I told David to ring for an ambulance as I continued to try and suction Annette. When David made contact with the ambulance service I took the phone. I explained that although I had just cancelled the previous call things had changed and we now wanted the ambulance as soon as possible.

Within a few minutes the ambulance had arrived. I continued to try to help Annette until the ambulance men took over. They tried to suction Annette, but to no avail. All this time Annette was conscious, though in a very distressed state. I was on the verge of panic as I watched the ambulance men. After failing to clear the tube the medics decided to bring Annette to Tallaght Hospital. They put a breathing apparatus on her and took her downstairs. I went in the ambulance with her and David followed in his car. She was whisked straight into the emergency room. The doctors started working on her immediately while I gave the details of her illness.

In all this time Annette had not lost consciousness, though later she said she did not remember the ambulance men treating her. After a few minutes of being suctioned with a tube similar to the one we had at home a larger one was brought in. This succeeded in clearing the large plug of mucus which was blocking Annette's tube. As soon as the mucus was dislodged Annette began to recover. Within five or six minutes she was almost back to normal. She did not remember much about the incident and thought she had been unconscious.

David, who had been waiting outside the emergency room, then came in. We waited until Annette had fully recovered and then we went home. Needless to say we did not go to St. Luke's that day as Annette was very tired after such a stressful morning. She rested for the rest of the day and seemed to be back to normal by evening time.

The events of the day cast a cloud over what had been a great weekend, but as Annette had recovered well from the experience and seemed to be ok again, we thought it was just a slight glitch in her recovery. We went to bed that night with plans to resume her treatment in St. Luke's the next day.

Annette had a reasonably good night after her stressful day and was fine the next morning. She got up and was ready without any bother. Her friend Maureen Monahan drove us to St. Luke's that Tuesday and the treatment went as normal.

Before we left the hospital we were asked to wait to see Annette's doctors. They had been informed about the previous day's events by Tallaght Hospital. After a short discussion with Annette the doctors suggested that in view of what had happened it would now be advisable for her to come into St. Luke's as an in-patient. They stressed this was not because she was any sicker, but just so that they could monitor her trachie tube and see what had caused the blockage. This was a blow to us after what had been said the previous Friday. But as Annette's well being and safety were paramount, she agreed to be admitted the following day.

That night she packed a bag to bring with her the following morning. Another friend of Annette's, Wally Maloney, drove us to St. Luke's on the Wednesday. On arrival Annette was allocated a room and, after settling in, she had her radiation treatment. She was back to herself again after Monday's events. I stayed with her until about nine o'clock that night. We took a walk around the hospital and visited the church. The Easter weekend was coming up and no treatment would take place from Good Friday to the following Tuesday. We had hoped that Annette could come home for the weekend after her Thursday sessions of chemo and radiation but the doctors felt it would be best if she stayed in, so they could keep a watch on her trachie tube.

I went down to St. Luke's at about ten o'clock on Thursday morning. I went straight to Annette's room, but she was not there, so I went to the chemo ward thinking she would be there. I was told by a nurse that she was still in the radiation dept. As I entered that section Annette was just coming out from her radiation treatment. She was in good form and told me she was getting the chemo in her own room, so we walked back there together.

David and Mina then came in to see her. Annette was very glad to see them but while they were there she started to have difficulty with her tube again. I called a nurse to give her aid. It did not seem as bad as on Monday, Annette was not having as much difficulty breathing nor was her colour changing. After the nurse attended to Annette she seemed to be ok again and we went back into the room.

After a while David had to leave but I was glad that Annette seemed to be alright again. She gave David and Mina a kiss before they left.

As Annette had had another blockage of her trachie a doctor had to see her before she could have her chemo. We had to wait for one to be available to check her. As we waited we spoke about the trouble the trachie was causing. Annette said she was not even thinking about the cancer, her whole concern was the trachie. She was afraid that it would become so blocked that it would not be possible to unblock it. The trachie nurse had assured us that this just would not happen, that it had never happened in the nine years she had been in the hospital. Eventually a doctor came and examined Annette. He said there was no reason for her not to have the chemo as everything seemed to be alright now. The doctor said he would go and get the line ready for the chemo. As he left the room Annette turned to me and uttered the last words I would ever hear her speak, "I think I'll go to the toilet first before they start." With those words Annette walked out of my life. She went into the bathroom as I sat on the bed to wait. After a moment or two I heard a banging noise from the bathroom. I ran in and found Annette holding the sink trying to get her breath.

I don't remember what happened next. I think I may have brought her out of the bathroom. All I remember is seeing Annette lying on the bed, surrounded by nurses as they tried to tend to her. Her head was propped up on a pillow and the nurses were trying to suction her. I remember looking at her as she seemed to fall into a state of unconsciousness. Her head dropped down on her right shoulder and her eyes were shut.

I was then pushed out of the room as more nurses and doctors came running from all directions. I was told to sit in a small room across from Annette's room. The door was open and I could see all the activity over at Annette's room. There were nurses and doctors going in and out, with equipment being brought in. I don't know how long all this went on, maybe half an hour.

Then Prof. Hollywood came into the room where I was waiting. He said he wanted to prepare me for the worst. He said that Annette might have had a cardiac arrest. They were not sure at that time but she was on a ventilator and when they took her off it she might not be able to breathe on her own. He said he just wanted to prepare me for what might happen. Prof. Hollywood was then called back to Annette's room leaving me alone to ponder over what he had just said, though I don't think I really fully comprehended it as my mind was really in the ward with Annette.

More activity began to take place. Nurses and doctors were running back and forward. I was left in the room alone. I tried to get into Annette's room to see her but I was prevented from doing so by a nurse who was standing just inside the door. Through all the people in the room I could just about see Annette lying on the bed. Then I was again taken back to the other room and told to wait there.

Another period of time passed before Prof. Hollywood came back to me. He said they were going to move Annette back to St. James's Hospital. They had taken her off the ventilator and she was continuing to breath unaided, but they did not have the facilities to treat her in St. Luke's. An emergency ambulance would arrive shortly to bring her to James's.

I asked Prof. Hollywood what had happened. He said he was not sure, it may have been a heart attack or it might have been a blockage of the trachie tube. They just did not know at that point but that it was best she was taken to St. James's. When the ambulance came I was not allowed to go with her. A taxi was called for me and as I waited for it to arrive I phoned David. I told him what had happened after he left and that Annette was on the way to St. James's. I think I may have called Gina and Robert but I am not sure.

The taxi took forever getting to St. James's, due to very heavy Holy Thursday traffic. I got out of the taxi at the roundabout in Rialto and ran the rest of the way because the traffic was at a standstill. As I ran towards the hospital gate I met David. He was also running, having parked his car further up the road.

As we made our way into the hospital I told him that things did not look too good. I explained that his Mam was unconscious when last I saw her and I did not know if they could do anything.

Annette was already in the emergency room when we got to the hospital and Gina and Robert were already there. They said they had seen her being taken in and she did not look good. We were not immediately allowed to see Annette. We were left waiting in a room outside. Gina or Robert had phoned Annette's family and very soon we were joined by Caroline, Claire, and Louis, followed shortly by Marie and her husband Maurice and her brother Liam.

After another while we were allowed into the emergency room, two at a time, to see Annette. She was unconscious but she looked relaxed and comfortable, not the least distressed or in pain. When we asked what had happened nobody seemed to know. We were told that Annette would be moved up to St. John's Ward as soon as possible. Further tests would then be carried out to determine what had happened.

What had started as an irritating sore throat was now a life threatening illness. I was totally shattered and confused, as I stood looking at Annette in her comatose state. Less than a week before we had been told she was doing so well that she could continue to attend St. Luke's as an out patient. What had gone wrong? Nobody seemed to know.

We were told to expect the worst by the medical team as they could do no more for Annette. They could only keep her pain free and comfortable but I still did not expect or believe Annette was going to die. I truly believed she would come out of this coma and continue her recovery. But that was not to be, it was just the blind refusal to accept reality of someone who does not want to lose the one he loves.

Later that evening Annette was moved to a room in St. John's ward. She remained there until her passing in the early hours of Easter Tuesday morning. The last four days of Annette's life were beautiful. She had a private room where all the family and her friends came to be with her and say their goodbyes.

Although we did not know if she could hear us or understand what we were saying, we stayed with her, played music, lit candles and said prayers.

After Annette was moved to St. Johns we were told she may have suffered brain damage, as she had stopped breathing for a time in St. Luke's. But we carried on as if she could hear and understand everything we were saying. We lit the room with candles and brought in lots of music, including her own compositions and some flowers. We made the room as much like home as we could.

The first piece of music Gina played was a piece by Mozart, whose music Annette loved. As the sound filled the room Annette responded by moving her right hand as if keeping time with the music. This was confirmation to us that she could indeed hear and understand what was happening. We talked to her all the time but we got no response back. Annette seemed to be paralysed on her left side, she did not move her left arm or leg at all after she was moved to St. John's ward.

We sent word to the rest of the family and to Annette's friends about what had happened. We told them they could come and visit Annette if they wished to do so. Over the next few days there was a constant stream of visitors saying goodbye to Annette.

On Easter Saturday night Annette's friend, Fr. Derek Farrell came to the hospital after he had celebrated Mass in his own church. He said prayers for Annette with David and me. He stayed talking with us for a while before he had to go.

After Fr. Farrell left Annette showed signs of uneasiness and began to move in the bed. I spoke to her and asked if she could hear me, but she continued to be uneasy. I thought she might be in pain so I asked her but I got no real response. She seemed to be trying to open her eyes. I thought she might be coming out of the coma, so I continued to speak to her and hold her hand. I again asked if she was in pain but Annette did not respond. She continued to move in the bed and her eyes opened once or twice.

I was concerned that she might be in pain and unable to let us know so I tried a new approach. I asked her to try to raise her little finger if she was in pain. Nothing happened. I then said if you are not in pain raise your little finger. Immediately her little finger shot up. I was delighted with this response, it meant she could hear what I was saying and she was not in any pain. It also meant she was not brain damaged.

I began to speak to Annette again now that I knew that she could hear and understand me. She seemed to relax and stopped moving around in the bed. I held her hand and told her everything that had happened. I said that Fr. Derek had been there and had prayed for her. David also spoke to her and when he had to go, he asked her for a kiss. Annette puckered her lips and tried to lift her face to be kissed by him. This was in the early hours of Easter Sunday and I began to believe that Annette was going to have a resurrection and come out of the coma she had gone into on Holy Thursday.

I stayed with her all night, talking and singing to her. I'm sure she could hear what I was saying. She held my hand in a firm grip and was very relaxed. I took the opportunity to tell her how much I loved her. I went over our life together, reminding her of all the good times we'd had and telling her there was going to be many more good times when she got better. I also told her how sorry I was for all the times I had hurt and disappointed her, promising never to do so again. I spoke, sang and kissed non-stop until the morning light brightened the room. Annette was completely relaxed when the nurse came in to check on her, early on Easter Sunday morning.

I stayed with Annette until the family came back about mid-morning. All Easter Sunday we had candles lighting and music playing in the room. We even had our lunch there just as if it was home. It was a beautiful atmosphere and Annette's sisters and friends came and visited during the day.

Later that day Annette lapsed back into the coma she had seemed to be coming out of the previous night. She did not respond to any words or to the music we played. The only consolation was she did not appear to be in pain or distressed in any way. To all intents and purposes she looked as if she was in a deep sleep.

That night Gina, David and Robert insisted that I go home for some sleep, but I did not want to leave Annette. I wanted to stay with her and do what I had done the previous night, talk and sing to her.

After protracted discussions I agreed to go home with Gina, on condition that I would stay with Annette on Monday night. But as we were on the way to Gina's house I changed my mind. I insisted that I wanted to go back to the hospital to be with Annette and Gina reluctantly brought me back. David stayed that night as well. We were given a room to sleep in and we took turns staying with Annette through the night.

Chapter Twenty Nine

By Easter Monday Annette was deep in a coma. She was completely unresponsive to all attempts to communicate with her. We continued to play her music and speak to her, but to no avail.

A very disturbing and distressing incident happened later that day. Up to Sunday, Annette had been on a drip to feed her, but when the feed was finished on Sunday night a new bottle of food was not put on. At first, we did not think much about this. We assumed that a new feed would come in a while. But by Easter Monday morning, no new food had been set up for Annette. We asked a nurse when Annette would be getting her food again, only to be told that the duty doctor had told the nurses not to set up Annette's feed again. This doctor was supposed to visit Annette that morning and speak to us, but he had not done so. He was also not a member of Dr Kinsella's team. I asked to see this doctor but he would not come back to the ward to speak to me so I asked a nurse to get him on the phone. When I challenged him on why he had issued instructions that Annette was not to be given any more food his response was that Annette had, "a very large tumour and would not get better." In other words he was about to let her die and not waste any more food on her.

I demanded to speak to this so-called doctor face-to-face but he would not come to the ward. This was maybe just as well, if he had come and repeated what he'd said so coldly to me on the phone I think he would have been in need of a doctor himself. He was not in the least helpful or sympathetic about our concerns. I demanded that he resume Annette's feed. He was reluctant to do so, citing "her large tumour" as a reason. I told this doctor what I thought of him and contacted Dr Kinsella. Although he was off duty that day, he came in and spoke to us.

Dr Kinsella was shocked by this turn of events, saying it should never have happened. He arranged for the food to be given to Annette immediately. This was a very distressing incident and one we should have pursued at the time. We should have confronted this doctor face-to-face, and made him explain his reason for withholding Annette's food, but because events soon over took us we did not take it further. I am sorry now that we did not do so. Doctors like that man are not fit to practice in our hospitals. He was totally desensitized to our distress and to Annette's condition. Annette had her family to speak up for her but how many other patients had this 'doctor' decided had lived long enough, especially if they had no one to speak up for them.

We told Dr Kinsella this man's name. I hope he spoke to him about his disgraceful behaviour, his lack of concern for patients and their families and reminded him of his Hippocratic Oath. Though after speaking to this man I doubt if it meant anything to him.

Dr Kinsella looked at Annette while he was in and told us she was very weak. In the gentlest way he told us that he did not think she would last much longer. At the prompting of the family he also told me to go home and get some rest as I would be no good to anyone if I collapsed through fatigue. I was still reluctant to leave Annette, especially if she did not have much longer to live. Though even then I did not fully believe she was going to die. I felt that she would prove all the doctors wrong by coming out of the coma and recovering.

As night fell pressure was again applied to me to go home and rest but I was resisting it. I wanted to stay. I pointed out that I would sleep for a while in the room provided to us by the hospital and I would be ok. However the family were still insisting that I go home. When Annette's friend Maureen Monahan, offered to stay with her and contact us if anything happened I gave in to the pressure and went home with Gina.

We went home at about ten o'clock on Easter Monday night and at 11.30 p.m., after about a half hour in bed we were summoned back to the hospital. When we got there Maureen was still with Annette, but we told her she could go now as we would stay for the rest of the night.

Annette's breathing was very shallow and there seemed to be long gaps between her breaths. I sat with her for a while, holding her hand and talking to her, but there was no response at all from her. She was almost gone from us.

The nurses on duty were monitoring her all the time. They told us it looked like the end was near. David, Gina and Robert told me to get a rest as I was out on my feet from lack of sleep and they would stay with Annette. I went into the rest room which was just up the hall and tried to doze off for a while.

I think I may have slept for an hour or so before I heard David call me. We rushed back to Annette's room just in time to be with her as she passed away from us, at 4.21 a.m. on Easter Tuesday morning.

To this day I do not fully remember Annette passing. I remember rushing into the room, and I am told I sat beside her and held her hand and spoke to her as she breathed her last, but it's all just a haze to me. It was a dreamlike state as we waited for the priest and doctor to come and pronounce Annette dead.

Looking back now, I don't believe I fully realised then that Annette was gone from us. I don't remember crying or even feeling sad, I was just going through the motions. The reality of what had happened had not sunk in. I remember leaving the hospital and going to Robert's house, but I was not fully comprehending what had happened. Annette was dead but it just had not registered with me at all. I felt quite normal and not at all perturbed by what had happened.

Later Robert and I went back to Raheen Green where David and Gina had arranged to meet the undertaker to plan Annette's funeral. I was still in a world of my own and did not fully understanding what was happening. I had no idea about where we should bury Annette, and it was Gina who suggested Bohernabreena to which I said yes, in all honesty if she had said Timbuktu I would probably have said yes as I was not functioning at all in a rational way. The fact that Annette was dead and we were planning her funeral did not penetrate my consciousness at all.

On Tuesday evening Gina and I went to the undertaker's premises in Aungier Street to see Annette laid out. I still did not comprehend what had happened. I was quite relaxed about it all. Gina had been nervous about seeing her mother laid out in a coffin but when we saw Annette she looked as if she was sleeping. She looked beautiful, with her hands clasped across her chest, holding her rosary beads. Gina was so happy to see how well Annette looked, she looked exactly like herself. When we came out of the undertakers, we went across the road to the Swan Bar. It was the bar myself and Gina, in her wedding dress, had had a drink in on the day of her wedding. We had been circling around waiting for David, her husband-to-be, to arrive at the church, the Unitarian Church on Stephens Green. As we had our drink after the undertakers, we remarked on the different circumstances prevailing then, to the sad occasion now.

We brought Annette home on Wednesday afternoon and laid her out in the front room, facing the mountains she loved. We filled the house with candles and played her music all the time. We did not want this time, the last day and night Annette would spend in her own home in Raheen Green, to be sad or depressing. She would not have wanted that. We wanted to celebrate her life and send her to her reward in a joyous way. She looked fantastic in the clothes Gina had picked for her final journey. I put her bible, a family picture and her passport into the coffin with her. I left her wedding ring on her finger because I will not let even death part us. We will be forever married, from here to eternity and when I go to join her I will be wearing my wedding ring.

All her friends and family came to say their final goodbyes to her and joined with us in celebrating her life. It was a life I was lucky to share and be part of for over forty years. On Thursday evening, after a day of rain which stopped long enough for us to walk the short distance to St. Mark's Church behind her coffin, Annette left her home in Raheen Green for the last time. The local gardai, mindful of how well known Annette was, provided an escort to the church. They stopped the traffic while the cortege passed the junction at Fortunestown Lane.

The short ceremony of accepting Annette's remains into the church was filled with music. The combined choirs of St. Mark's church and the Priory Prayer Group, of which Annette was a member, played and sang. This would have pleased Annette very much.

After the ceremony the extended family came back to the house. We had a glass of wine and toasted Annette's life. Robert stayed with me the night before the funeral and early the next morning Gina, David, Ciara and Dave came down. I had asked the choirs to play as much of Annette's music as they could fit into the funeral Mass. They played and sang four of Annette's songs: *With you Beside me, The Breastplate, Windows of Your Soul and To The Ends of The Earth.* Just before the Mass started and with the permission of Fr. Gerard Doyle, the local curate, I played a recording of Annette herself singing one of her songs, *When the Summer Comes Round Again.* As Annette was taken from the church I had a recording of Frank Sinatra singing "From Here to Eternity" played. Only later did I realise that Sinatra was there at both the beginning and the end of our earthly relationship.

The Mass was celebrated by Annette's friend, Fr. Derek Farrell. He gave a very personal and moving eulogy. Fr Farrell spoke of Annette's generosity, her sincerely held beliefs, her concern for people, especially those who were marginalised or excluded and her achievements.

After the mass Annette was laid to rest in Bohernabreena Cemetery, near the mountains she loved. The family and many of her friends came back with us to the Plaza Hotel for a light lunch. Music was provided by Tom Quinn, the friend who was involved in the "Nighthawks" show with me in November 2008. The night at which I now believe my mother had forewarned me about Annette's death, but at the time I did not understand her words.

Chapter Thirty

After Annette's passing I was numb for a few days. I still did not fully realise what had happened. But then, when it was all over and I was in the house alone, the walls caved in. Only then did the magnitude of what had happened hit me. When everyone was gone and I was surrounded with quietness and solitude my tears burst forth and my loss overwhelmed me. The children wanted me to stay with them, but I just wanted to be alone in the house, with my memories.

When the reality of what had happened hit me I was grief-stricken, and it was then that the strange but comforting things started to happen. On the second Saturday after Annette's passing I was having a particularly bad day. I had heard people say in the past, that after a loved one died they had felt their presence all around them. But since her passing I could not feel Annette's presence, not at all. I had not even dreamt about her.

That Saturday I was crying and calling on Annette to let me have some kind of a sign that she was still around and all right. I was desperate for a sign. Something I cried, anything, a sign to let me know she was not just a memory.

The day dragged and later that night, as I was about to go up to bed, I was sitting on the couch gazing at the blank TV screen. I had just turned it off when I heard a light "plop" sound. It was the sound of something hitting Annette's tambourine which was on a bookshelf across the room. I looked in that direction and saw a sheet of paper on top of the tambourine. I don't know how long this piece of paper had been on the shelf. I did not even know what it was or what was on it.

I got off the chair and went over to the tambourine. Sitting on top of it, as if it had been carefully placed there, was the sheet of paper. On top of the paper was a small, white, carefully folded handkerchief which Annette had at some time in the past brought home from Medugorje. I picked it up and looked at what was written on the sheet of paper:

Let it go
Let it go my friend
Just let it go and never look back
Let it go my friend
Let me be the one to set you back on the track
My friend you can depend on me
Let it go my friend
There's nothing you need to be frightened of
And you know my friend in the midst of your pains you'll
experience my love
My friend you can depend on me
Place your trust in me,
I'll guide you all the way, why even the blind can see and
the deaf hear
what I say
Let it go my friend
Let go of the pain; let go of the hurt
Time will show you my friend
I already know how much you're worth
My friend you can depend on me

How the piece of paper and handkerchief managed to fall as they did was a mystery. There was no breeze and the windows were closed. After reading the prayer I put them back on the shelf. I tried to make them fall onto the tambourine in the same way, but, try as I might it was not possible to do so, unless I placed them on the tambourine by hand. Every time I let them fall from the shelf they fell separately onto the floor, well away from the tambourine. Was Annette answering my cries of despair?

This was the first of a series of strange occurrences that followed Annette's passing. All of them were a great comfort to me, and they were all inexplicable. By nature I was a sceptic and a cynic, and I had little, indeed no faith in organised religion. I had been born a Catholic but I did not practice it or any religion. I had not done so for over thirty years. Even when I did go, it was without much conviction. I just went to Mass with

Annette and the kids on a Sunday morning and sat there bored until it was over. At one time this was a huge issue between us, as Annette was a committed Christian all her life. She felt I should have given the children a better example and backed her up when they began to neglect their faith during their teenage years. But I could not tell them to do something I was not doing or did not believe in myself. Over the years we had gradually come to accept and respect each other as the people we were and got on with life.

Though I did not believe in religion, I very much believed in a power greater than humanity. I did not go along with the proposition that it was all down to "the big bang" and evolution. I felt and believed that even if science could prove "the big bang" had taken place eons ago, someone or something had to have pressed the button to set it off. Nothing happens in a vacuum of its own accord. Likewise with evolution, while certain changes in species could be traced over millions of years, I believed that there had to be a "designer" to oversee the changes. I believed that chance and coincidence could only account for so much of the changes, and that would be on the outside. The evolution of the brain, the nervous system and the subconscious was another thing altogether. It was something that had to be carefully overseen and planned and not left to chance. Right or wrong these were my beliefs and the theories of good and evil, God and the Devil, Heaven and Hell put forward as beliefs by organised religion had no part in them.

I am setting out my beliefs to show where I was in terms of faith at the time of Annette's passing and the amount of credence I gave to orthodox Christian beliefs about life after death. If, before Annette's passing, I had been asked if I believed in a life after death, my reply would have been along the lines of, "I don't know or care if there is one or not, I have no fears or expectations. Whatever is there is there and I have no control over it". But since Annette's passing I know and believe beyond doubt that life goes on in some shape or form after we depart this life. That's why I try not to use the word death when speaking of Annette's passing from this life. Too many things have happened that cannot be explained, or cannot be explained away by reference to imagination or coincidence, and I believe they started on the night of 2nd November, 2008. After the incident of the falling poem and handkerchief a number of other strange things happened. The first was about a week later when Gina came to visit, with Senan and Ella-May. We had not said anything about Annette's passing to the grandchildren, beyond saying that Nana had gone to live with the angels. We felt they were too young to take it in and it would have been too painful for them. The grandchildren were not at Annette's funeral either. When they arrived, as it was a fine day, we decided to take the children to the new playground which had recently opened in the park near the village. As Gina drove to the playground she asked me if I would like to visit the cemetery first. I said yes.

Without saying anything to Senan and Ella, who were in the back seat of the car playing with toys, Gina drove to the cemetery. As we approached the gates she prepared to drive in. Now remember the children had never been there before and they had been told they were going to the new playground, but Ella perked up on the seat in the back of the car and said: "Nana lives here." We were so shocked and amazed by what we thought we had heard that we asked her what she had said. She repeated: "Nana lives here."

About a week after this I had the first of a series of what I have referred to as "thought intrusions". By this I mean thoughts which do not originate in my own mind, but seem to come from outside, in the form of a communication from Annette. I have already referred to the "get your feet off me" incident, the "clutter" and "ghost writer" intrusions while I was in the cemetery.

This kind of "thought intrusion" has happened on a number of other occasions, I have also had other indications that Annette is still exerting her influence from wherever she is now . On the day of the 45th anniversary of our first meeting I went to Bray and went to the spot where we first met. I had asked Annette if it was at all possible for her to do so, to let me know that she remembered what day it was. Nothing happened in Bray but later that night when I went home I was flicking through the t.v. channels and at approximately 8-15 p.m, the time we would have been in the Capitol cinema back in 1965 watching *Von Ryan's Express* a caption from a t.v. channel I do not subscribe to came on the screen, the film being shown? *Von Ryan's Express*! after a moment I flicked to the next channel, again one I do not subscribe to and a caption came onto the screen with the words *You Can Depend On Me,* a coincidence?, maybe, but I was very comforted by it and I felt Annette was still around somewhere.

Shortly after this incident, on the night of 16th of August I could not sleep and was tossing around in the bed at approximately 1-50 a.m. when a very strong notion came into my mind to turn on the bedside radio, when I did a female voice I recognised but could not identify was singing. When the song ended the presenter announced the singer as Pauline Scanlon, the daughter of Paul Scanlon from Dingle. Did Annette want me to hear her?

One more example of Annette's influence on events since her passing was when I was arranging for a headstone to be erected on the grave. I was undecided between two photographs of Annette and didn't know which one to put on the headstone. I took them both down to the monumental sculptors one morning to get advice on which photograph I should use. I had the two pictures in a bag in which I also had a bunch of flowers to put on the grave. I explained my predicament to the lady in the office and she asked to see them. As I took the flowers out of the bag so I could get at the pictures one of them came out with the flowers and landed on the table between us. Both of us looked at the picture and I just said: "That's the one." It was a picture of Annette sitting on the Fungi statue in Dingle.

Another strange thing happened on our son David's birthday, the 19th of June 2009. It was the first family birthday Annette would not be there for and we were all a bit emotional in the days coming up to it. I was in the house alone that day, sitting reading the paper in the front room when the chimes which we have hanging in the hall started to gently ring. Now this does not happen unless the door is opened as the chimes are moved by the door. I had not noticed anyone coming up the driveway so I was surprised. I went out to the hall to see who was coming in but there was nobody there and the door was closed. There was no breeze and the windows were closed, but as I stood looking at the chimes they continued to ring, very gently for about a minute or so. Was this Annette saying she had not forgotten David's birthday?

Stranger still was what happened two days later, on Sunday, 21st June, Father's Day. I woke up feeling very sorry for myself as Annette had always given me a little something on that day, a bottle of wine or a naggin of whiskey or something like that, and I did the same for Annette on Mother's Day. But this Father's Day I would be getting nothing from Annette. It was a very misty and damp day and as I sat alone eating my breakfast. I was contemplating whether I should go to the cemetery or not when a thought came into my mind: 'go to the cemetery and bring something religious.' I was puzzled by this, what was this about, go to the cemetery and bring something religious? Where was that coming from? I did not understand it. I was not in the least religious and to bring something religious with me was the last thing I would think of doing. But the thought persisted and seemed to be repeating itself.

After breakfast I was still undecided about whether to go to the cemetery or not as the weather was damp and misty but I could not get the thought out of my mind so I decided to go. I looked around for something religious to bring with me and settled on a small Divine Mercy candle holder and candle. I put it into my saddle bag and cycled off to the cemetery.

As I reached the Mill Pub and was about to turn up the road to the cemetery all at once I knew what 'bring something religious' meant . It suddenly hit me that it was the day of the annual cemetery mass and Annette wanted something of a religious nature on her grave for it. I was delighted and amazed that Annette had communicated with me in this way and on this day. When I got to the cemetery I was able to decorate her grave with fresh flowers for the Mass, as there was a flower seller outside the gates.

Things did not end there. I was only home about twenty minutes when there was a knock on the door. As I was preparing a light lunch for the children who were coming to visit me for Father's Day, at first I thought they were early. But when I opened the door I was very surprised to see our former neighbours, Mary and Mike Cabazon standing outside. They had lived in the house next door to us for many years but had moved some years before and rented out their house. I had last seen them at Annette's funeral and before that when Annette was attending St. Luke's and we spoke to them while they were renovating the house for some new tenants.

As I stood looking at them, with a surprised look on my face, I noticed that Mike had a very strange and emotional look on his face. I asked them in and we went into the front room. As we stood looking at each other, each as uncomprehending as the other, Mike almost broke down as he said: "Andy, your wife saved my life."

I did not know what he meant. All I could do was look at him and say: "I don't understand Mike. What do you mean?"

Mike then pulled down his coat collar and I was shocked to see he had a line of stitches, exactly like the stitches I had seen on Annette's neck after her operation. Mike went on to explain that when he had last spoken to Annette he had mentioned that he had a small lump on his neck which had been there for a long time, but it did not bother him in any way. Annette told him he should have it seen to. He did not do anything about it until after Annette had passed away but then he remembered what she had said. He went to see a doctor who sent him for some tests. The results showed he had thyroid cancer.

He had been referred to St. James's Hospital where he was seen by Dr. Kinsella, Annette's doctor. Dr Kinsella asked him why he had decided to have the lump on his neck looked at now and Mike told him that a neighbour of his had recently died from cancer and she had told him to go and have it seen to before she died. Dr. Kinsella asked who the neighbour was and

Mike mentioned Annette's name. Dr. Kinsella then told Mike that he knew Annette as he had treated her. He also told him he had come just in time. If he had let it go any longer he would have been in very great danger.

Mike became emotional as he told me this. He is convinced that Annette is responsible for him being alive. He would not have done anything about the lump had he not spoken to her. Before they left Mike handed me a bottle of wine as a gift. So, a morning which had started with me feeling sorry for myself because I thought I would not be getting a present from Annette for Father's Day ended with me getting two, a communication from Annette, and she also managed to get me a bottle of wine. Just one more thing about Mike Cabazon, he shares the same birthday as Annette, 13th August.

CHAPTER THIRTY ONE

I've referred to the night of 2nd November in the Plaza Hotel Tallaght before. Now I want to go into those events and what followed in greater detail. After Annette had been diagnosed with cancer I made an effort to try and find out who the lady was who had approached me in the Plaza on the night of November 2nd With the assistance and help of my friend Alan Fitzpatrick I succeeded in learning that the lady was a medium named Joan Glennon, although she had told me on the night that she was a medium she had not mentioned her name. She was in the Plaza that night as a guest of the hotel's Assistant Manager, Karl Walker. She was a friend of his parents. I obtained her phone number through Alan Fitzpatrick. Alan contacted Karl Walker for me as Karl had left the hotel and was living and working in Mayo.

After Annette became seriously ill in the New Year I had wondered about that night and what had been said, particularly because of the pictures falling and cracking at home. I wondered about the implications that could be read into that, as it had happened on my mother's anniversary, and the medium had said that my mother was holding up a watch. To perhaps signify that time was running out for us? Something about a throat had also been mentioned and now Annette was suffering with throat cancer. But I hesitated about contacting her as I was spending so much time in the hospital with Annette. Then after Annette passed away there did not seem much point. But because of what had happened in Bohernabreena Cemetery on the morning of 24th July I felt I now had no choice, I had to make contact with her. I had to try and get some explanation for the things she had said on 2nd November, 2008.

I rang her on Sunday, 26th July after thinking long and hard about it. I identified myself and asked if she remembered meeting me in the Plaza Hotel the previous November. She said she did, so I then said that certain things had happened in relation to what she had said that night and I would like to speak to her about them. I did not mention that Annette had passed away. She said that she could see me the following Friday, at 11.30 a.m., in her house in Blessington. I said I would be there.

The series of strange incidences which had occurred after Annette's passing – Ella saying "Nana lives here" as we went to the cemetery, the letter falling from the shelf, the chimes ringing of their own accord on David's birthday, my communications from Annette and the visit of Mary and Mike Cabazon, and his conviction that Annette was responsible for saving his life, all seemed to lead up to what happened in Bohernabreena cemetery on the morning of Friday, 24th July. That morning convinced me that I should get in touch with the lady who had approached me in the Plaza Hotel the previous November.

One of the things that had been said that night was a complete mystery to me. I just could not understand it. I had talked it over with the family and none of us could understand it, it did not make any sense. The lady had asked me if I was interested in gardening and I replied not in the slightest. She had then said something about roses and that my mother was standing behind me, plucking thorns from a rose. We just could not figure that one out.

Before Annette's grave had a headstone, I used to put the flowers, usually roses, into one of the vases on the grave. On Friday morning, 24th July, I brought flowers to the grave for the first time since the headstone had been erected. The headstone had two flower pots with metal tops on it, one on each side of the plinth so I took the vases off the grave. I wanted to reduce the clutter now that there was a headstone. I had bought two bunches of roses, one for each flower pot. I unwrapped the flowers and began to put them into the pots, but because of the small holes in the metal grills the roses would not go in. The thorns were protruding from the stems of the flowers so I began to take them off. It was only when I had inserted about three roses that I realised what I was doing. I was plucking the thorns from the roses.

It was too close to what Joan Glennon had said in the Plaza the previous November to be a coincidence, so there and then I rang Gina and told her what I was doing. It seemed like we at last knew the full implication of what my mother had been trying to tell us. After I spoke to the family I decided I had to get in touch with Joan Glennon. Too much had happened since last November that could not be explained.

On Friday, 31st of July, I went to keep my appointment with Joan Glennon in Blessington. Joan had said she would pick me up from the bus stop as her house might be difficult to find. I arrived early and tried to make my own way to her home but I was misdirected and couldn't find her house. I had to phone her and ask for directions. It turned out I was not too far from her home so Joan told me to keep walking and she would come and pick me up.

When we got to Joan's home we went into her study. I again asked Joan if she remembered meeting me in the Plaza Hotel the previous November and if she remembered what she had said to me that night. She said she did indeed remember meeting me, but she did not remember what she had said, as she does not remember any of her consultations afterwards. She said she remembered the night because she does not normally approach people on a night out and give communications, but she felt compelled to do so that night.

I then reminded her of what she had said to me but I did not mention, nor had I mentioned on the phone that Annette had passed away. After telling her what she had said to me, I said that certain things had happened since that night and I was wondering if she could in any way clarify what she had said, now that I had reminded her of her words.

She said she was afraid she could not help me as she still did not remember.

I then felt I had no choice but to tell her why I had got in contact with her now. I said that since last November my wife, and I did not mention Annette's name, had passed away from cancer which had started in her throat. I told her of how I found myself plucking the thorns from the rose as she had said my mother was doing.

She expressed surprise that Annette had died and asked me if she had been the lady sitting beside me that night. When I said yes, Joan said how well she had looked that night. Then she suddenly seemed to change tack. She said, "I'm getting Ann. Ann is coming through."

As Ann is not a million miles from Annette I said, "My wife's name is Annette."

Joan continued to speak. She said she had to tell me that Annette was very happy now where she was and then she said something that rocked me,

"She says she is very happy about the car." and before I got over that shock, she continued, "She loves the poem you wrote for her and is glad you changed the inscription on the tombstone."

She also said, " She says our love will never die, she'll always be with you."

I had decided before going to see Joan that I would say as little as possible so I would not lead her in any way. As she spoke I did not respond to what she was saying, but just let her talk, without indicating if she was making sense or not.

Joan then said some things which I could not relate to as they had no meaning for me. But she continued, "You made the right choice about the photograph."

She went on to speak about Annette's passing, "She says she was glad it was quick, as she did not have time to think about it and that she had not been in pain and passed peacefully. She was glad she died when she did, she was very happy with the send off you gave her and the way she was dressed." She also said Annette was saying something about "Frank or Frankie" and about "Showtime".

I may be reading more into this than I should, but I had been working on a one man show about Frank Sinatra. After Annette passed away I had decided to stop the project as I just did not feel I could give it the attention it needed. Hearing this I thought just maybe Annette was encouraging me to continue with it. In the event she did encourage me and I have resumed work on it.

Then as Joan finished she said something that at the time just did not register with me at all. Maybe because I was still in a state of wonderment at the things I was hearing, a lot of which I could relate to, the car, the inscription, the photograph, the poem and the quick and peaceful way Annette had passed over. Joan finished by saying that Annette said I used to have problems with my knees but she had: "fixed it for me."

When I got on the bus to go home I wrote down everything about the session, I did not want to forget anything so I wrote it all of down as soon as I could. As I read over my notes the following day it hit me that my knees, which had indeed been a problem, especially when climbing stairs or sitting down for a period of time, were now working perfectly. It had been a number of weeks since I had last had problems climbing stairs, certainly six or seven. In fact I had forgotten about it. When Annette was alive, and I was struggling to get up or down the stairs, holding tight to the banister as my knees stiffened, she used to tell me to go and see about my knees or I was liable to end up a cripple. Unlike Mike Cabazon, I did not heed her warning, so she took action herself and now my knees are fine.

When Annette said: "She was happy about the car," this refers to her car. I do not drive, and after Annette passed away David and Gina urged me to learn. They wanted me to use Annette's car which was lying outside in the driveway, but I had no real interest in cars or driving. To please them I said I would take some driving lessons and see if I wanted to drive. In May I took a series of driving lessons, but I just was not interested. The car, an o3 Citroën in good condition, was just lying outside unused. When I decided I did not want to drive I asked David, Gina and Robert if any of them wanted it. They were all happy with the cars they had and declined the offer. All of Annette's sisters, with the exception of Marie and her youngest sister Louise had cars. Marie's husband, Maurice, drives her anywhere she wants to go but Annette had often commented on the fact that Louise had to bring her daughters, Shannon and Ceilie, to camogie, and anywhere else they had to go, by bus, and Annette wished Louise had a car of her own to get around. I told David, Robert and Gina if they did not want Mam's car I was going to offer it to Louise. They all thought that was a good idea, so that's what I did, I gave Louise Annette's car. When Joan Glennon said that Annette was "very happy about the car" I was flabbergasted. There was no way Joan could have known what that meant. She did not know if I had a car or not as I had come by bus.

Likewise with my knees, if I had been stumbling down the road or walked with the aid of a stick she might have had reason to suspect that I had problems with my legs, but I was walking smartly towards her when she came to meet me. She had also referred specifically to my knees which was my problem, not in general terms to my legs.

Concerning the inscription I had indeed changed the wording on the headstone. I had told the sculptors I wanted the words "Memories never die" to be inscribed, but I had changed my mind. Instead I asked for "As long as there are memories, love lives on" to be set on the top of the head stone and "All is well." to be put on the bottom. It was a phrase Annette was fond of using in times of stress. I asked for this to be done the day before the work was due to start. Again there was no way Joan could have known this.

Likewise with the reference to the photograph and me "making the right choice" how did she know if there was a photograph on the headstone at all?

The poem that she said Annette loves can only be the one I wrote for her memorial card.

I did not comment on any of the things Joan said until she was finished. Then I told her the significance of everything she had said.

Joan did say other things which made no sense to me. She also failed to mention a word I had asked Annette to say when I told her I was going to see Joan. It was a word whose meaning was known only to the two of us. I would have been convinced beyond all doubt that Annette was still around if she had spoken that word, but over all I was impressed. I could directly relate to about eighty per cent of what Joan had said, and while I did not understand the rest, who is to say time will not bring forth its meaning.

It's now over nine months since the night in the Plaza Hotel when all this started, over four months since Annette passed away, and events are still happening. Only last week I was in the cemetery with Gina and as I tended to Annette's grave Gina was walking around looking at other graves. I happened to look up at her and she had a stunned look on her face. I asked her what was the matter and she said she had "heard" Mam saying to her: "Is it me you came to see or what?"

CHAPTER THIRTY TWO

It's Wednesday, 2nd of September, 2009.

Last night I came back from Dingle having spent the weekend there. I was relinquishing our ownership of the old mobile that had played such a big part in our life for the past eleven years. It was a particularly sad time for me giving up the old mobile, but all things must come to an end and Dingle without Annette was just unthinkable. David, Ciara and Mina came with me and we spent Friday and Saturday night in the Dingle Skellig Hotel. When they left on Sunday they dropped me down to the mobile. I spent Sunday and Monday nights there. I wanted to do this. I wanted to sleep in the little bedroom again, before giving it up. I brought down Annette's CD so I could hear her voice one more time in the mobile, but for the first time ever the CD player would not work.

I walked around Dingle visiting all the places Annette used to love to go to. I went into the church, which she always made a point of visiting, and I lit a few candles. I also arranged to have a Mass said for her, which I'm sure she would be very happy about. I walked along the harbour and looked at the Fungi statue. I imagined Annette sitting on it, as she is in the picture on her headstone. I sat on Bin Bann beach on Monday and wept as I looked at the text messages we had sent each other during her illness.

On Monday night I went to John Benny's bar and had a meal alone. After it I said my goodbyes to Yvonne, the girl who had served us many times in the past, and to John. Then I headed up the road to the Global Village restaurant to tell Nuala the sad news about Annette and to say goodbye but the restaurant was closed. I went to the Droichead Beag where we had spent many happy nights together, listening to the music. I had one pint in the Droichead and then phoned Kathleen Curran, the lady with the taxi who had driven us home at the end of many happy nights in the past. Kathleen did not know Annette had passed away and she was surprised to see me standing on the bridge waiting for her on my own. When I got into the car I told Kathleen about Annette and she, like everyone else, was shocked and saddened by the news.

When I got back to the mobile I said my goodbyes to Paul and Eileen Scanlon and finished the bottle of wine I had brought with me. I packed a few items I wanted to keep from the mobile, and for the last time, I went to sleep in the little bed alone. In the past I had so often snuggled close to Annette in it as we slept a contented sleep after a night out in Dingle, but that night I only had my memories to cling to.

Kathleen drove me to the bus the next morning and after eleven very happy years in Dingle it was all over.

Everything I have written and recorded in this memoir is true, all I have related about Annette, the night in the Plaza, her passing and the things that happened after her passing happened just as I have written them. From time to time I go over the events in my mind as I sit alone in the house. I question everyone of them, forensically querying what exactly happened on each occasion. I am always left with the startling knowledge and certainty that each incident did indeed happen.

This is very comforting to me as I am now sure that Annette is in a place where she is happy and contented, and from where, every once in a while, she can still keep in touch with those she has left behind. But I am still sleeping alone in the big empty bed, still eating alone and still very lonely for Annette's company. I still crave her physical presence, her touch, her voice, but most of all her company. I still wake up each morning knowing I will not see or touch my wife today.

My life has changed completely since Annette's passing. We did everything together, we were one and now there is a huge part of me missing. I find it strange now going places on my own. Even going to visit the children is not the same as it once was. I'm on my own now with no one to bounce remarks or ideas off or crack a joke with about something or other. Walking around the Square in Tallaght brings back all kinds of memories. I can "see" Annette everywhere in it, as she acknowledged greetings and stopped to talk to the many friends she always met as we went around the shops.

One of the hardest things to do since Annette went out of my life is to come back to the house alone and enter an empty, cold house. Whenever we went out socially we always had a glass of wine and a chat about the night when we came home, and I miss that very much now. Earlier I wrote about the freedom I now have to do whatever I want, whenever I want around the house, but it's very strange having the run of the house, and to be free to live among my clutter knowing Annette is not going to be on to me about it. I still think of the house as Annette's and the things in it as belonging to her. Even though she is no longer here I'm still very careful of 'her' delph, 'her' glasses, 'her' cosmetics in the bathroom, and even of the few clothes of hers I have kept in the wardrobe. I am careful to see they are not creased. Although I know it's foolish and will not happen, I still half expect her to come walking in the door with a big smile on her face, and if she does I want the place to be as she would want it to be.

I have taken off the last sheets Annette and I lay on in the bed. I have replaced them with fresh sheets, but I have not washed them, nor do I intend to do so. They are folded carefully on a shelf of the bookcase in the bedroom, and that's where they will stay as long as I am in the house. They contain the only part of Annette not in the grave, her smell. I intend to keep that smell in the bedroom with me until I die.

Without Annette I am only half alive and although I go through the motions of day-to-day living my heart is not in it. I've resumed work on my Frank Sinatra show, but quite honestly I don't care if it comes to fruition or not. The only thing I am putting any effort into is this memoir as I believe Annette is still with me while I'm working on it.

I try to remind myself as I wake up each morning without Annette that it's not one day longer since I last saw and held her, but one day nearer the time I will do so again. My beliefs on what happens after passing from this life have changed. I am now convinced that death is not the end, but just a passing into another plain of existence, where the soul or spirit, or whatever name you like to put on it, continues to exist.

I was a very sceptical person before November 2008 and did not have any beliefs or cares at all about what happened after death, but I cannot ignore all that has happened, nor can I put it down to coincidence or chance. The things said to me by Joan Glennon were too personal and too true not to have been told to her by anyone other than Annette. No one else had that knowledge, certainly not Joan Glennon.

I go to the cemetery most evenings and talk to Annette. I talk to her about the things that have happened that day, about the family, about this memoir that I continually remind her she is writing with me, after all she did say she would be "my ghost writer". I tell her how far we are with it and continue to ask for her help and guidance in writing it. I tell her that I am hearing her prompts as I try to remember the details of our forty four years together. I tell her how much I love her and how lonely it is without her.

Most times I get no response, but now and again I 'hear' Annette responding to my words, and I know that "all is well."

EPILOGUE

It is over two years now since Joan Glennon approached me in the Plaza Hotel and related to me a message from my mother that I did not at the time understand. I still do not understand why I was singled out to be given that message when I was incapable and powerless to do anything about the consequences.

It has been a very strange and sad time for me and the family since then, life without Annette is lonely beyond explanation. My life has changed profoundly. I cannot begin to put into words how desolate and lonely I feel at times and how, as hard as I try to convey otherwise, meaningless and empty my life is now without Annette's presence in my life. For almost forty-four years Annette was my companion and best friend. She was beside me in everything I did and I was beside her. Now it feels as if more than half of me is missing; I am incomplete without her.

Two years ago our forty-four years together began to unravel and it was over in less than six months. All we had and all we had done in those forty-four years is now just a series of ghostly memories. I keep trying to conjure them up in my mind and relive them again, but try as I might that is not possible. The best I can do is to bring to mind visions of places we visited together and imagine Annette's smiling face looking at me. To help me in this task, since Annette's passing I have filled the walls of the staircase and landing with pictures taken of her in the places we visited during the many holidays we took. I have also hung up many pictures of Annette, taken during her year as Tallaght Person of the Year, back in 1991. It's really remarkable how little Annette changed or aged, apart from the colour of her hair, in those eighteen years.

Annette's physical presence is gone from my life for ever. All the things we once did together I now have to do alone, I eat alone, I watch TV alone, I visit friends and family alone, and saddest of all, I climb the stairs to the big empty bedroom alone each night and wake up each morning to the silence of an empty house, alone. This is the hardest and saddest part of my life now. I heard Mary O'Rourke, the T.D speaking on the radio some time ago of her loneliness in the early morning and at bedtime. I know exactly what she means, I endure this ordeal every day, and it does not get any easier.

It is now November and the long dark evenings are upon us again and Christmas beckons. It is a Christmas I am dreading and even at this remove I wish it was over. It will be the second time in forty-five years I will not go shopping for a Christmas present for Annette, the second time in forty-two years that Annette and I will not share a drink and a cuddle on Christmas Eve and sample the just cooked turkey and ham on fresh bread sandwiches with liberal amounts of Coleman's Mustard, and then, tired and happy, climb the stairs to bed and wake up in each others arms on Christmas morning.

Christmas was a favourite time of the year for us, we both loved all the festivities, meeting our friends and family, buying the Christmas tree and decorating the house with lights and tinsel. In later years we loved having our children and their partners up to the house for Christmas dinner. In the last few years we had begun to bring our grandchildren to the panto, just as we had done when our own children were young.

But all that is changed and will be forever more. Annette was such a lively and vibrant person, even in the early stages of her illness, that it is still so hard to believe she is gone, I find it hard to say the word dead because I still cannot think of Annette as being "dead" but she is gone. Last year when Gina and I attended the Mass of All Souls in St. Mark's church to remember all who died in the parish in the past year, when Annette's name was called it was proof positive that my beloved wife had left my side in this life for good.

During the course of the Mass the priest spoke about our loved ones passing over to a new life and us being reunited with them again when we died. Two years ago I would have scoffed at this, but what I have experienced since Annette passed away has changed my thinking completely. I am totally convinced that Annette or her spirit, her consciousness, her soul, call it what you will, is still alive and is still out there somewhere, and, from time to time, is able to communicate across whatever dimensions or divisions separate us.

It is this knowledge that now sustains me in my days of loneliness, the knowledge that I will be with, and will see, Annette again.

In the two years since Annette's passing I have gone back to visit Bray where we first met on a sunny August Sunday in 1965 and stood at the spot where we met. From there I gazed across the expanse of sea to where the Khyber Pass Hotel once stood in Dalkey, where we held our wedding reception. I tried to visualise Bullock Harbour and the Shangri-La restaurant where we danced away many a night when we were a young and carefree courting couple, but my tears obstructed the view. I attempted to have a drink in the Bray Head Hotel, where we had our first meal and drink as husband and wife, but the day I was there renovations were going on and the bar was closed.

In my mind I have relived our life together, over and over again. It torments me that it all ended so suddenly, so quickly and so unexpectedly, that when the cancer came it came so quietly that it ambushed us and caught us completely off guard. Cancer was something that happened to other people, not to us. I feel cheated that our time together was extinguished just when we were so happy and had the time and the money to begin to do and see many of the things that had eluded us earlier in our lives. I feel that the golden years we should have had together were stolen, the memories that had yet to be created and stored away for reminiscing in our old age with our grandchildren will now never be. I feel so sad that Annette will not be with her grandchildren as they grow into adulthood. I grieve for them that they have lost and will not have the love, wisdom and guidance Annette, their Nana, would have given them as they grew into young adults. For our children, David Gina and Robert, I am so sorry they will not have their mother's shoulder for comfort, when, as is inevitable, they are confronted with life's troubles.

Annette's passing has been a cross for us all that we will have to carry for the rest of our lives. She was such a huge and powerful presence in our lives, a gigantic source of love and compassion for all, which I know can never be replaced.

After Annette's passing some of her friends asked me what I intended to do with her music. Some of her friends knew she composed songs and some only became aware of her music at her funeral Mass. Those who heard her music for the first time were surprised and impressed with her talent. I had thought about it and I did intend to try and do something with her compositions. I approached her friends and work colleagues in South Dublin County Council with an idea that would I hoped keep Annette's name and memory alive and help other young musicians to develop their talents and careers. Arts Officer Orla Scannell and her assistants, Collette Ryan and Blaithin Keegan, immediately agreed to help me with this idea.

Annette had often commented about how little help was available to young up and coming musicians in Tallaght, so I thought it would please her very much if her music could be used to help and encourage others. I put my idea to Orla and she fell in with it immediately. She arranged to make the Civic Theatre in Tallaght available for a concert of Annette's music in March 2010. All proceeds from the night to be given to South Dublin County Council to set up some kind of a fund or foundation in Annette's name to be used to help young musicians develop their talent. I was given two dates on which the Civic was available, the 15th or the 27th of March and I asked Annette to help me decide on the best date for the concert.

On Thursday, 22nd October 2009, I was telling Annette about the concert as I stood at her grave. I was asking for her help and guidance in organising it and deciding on the best date when a man I used to work with in HB ice cream approached me. I had not seen Liam since leaving HB in 2002. We spoke for a while and Liam told me his wife had died the previous year. She was buried just up beyond Annette.

When Liam went on his way I got a notion to go and visit his wife's grave. I went in search of it and after a while I found it.

When I looked at the headstone the first thing I noticed was the date of the lady's death, 27th March, 2008. Was Annette telling me the date for her concert?

The concert was a great success, we filled the Civic and 3000 euro was raised which went to help two young violinists take master classes in France and a local rock band complete a C.D of their music. It could not have been done without the help and encouragement of many of Annette's friends who rowed in behind me and agreed to perform her music on the night. I owe a great debt of gratitude to Fr. Derek Farrell and the Traveller Choir, The Priory Prayer Group Choir, St Marks Parish Choir, John Carpenter, Shirley Whelan, Ray Flanagan, Pat Good, Liam Kennedy, Tony Lawless, Glenn Bainton, Alan Fitzpatrick and Indi Band, Junah who all gave their time and talents. I took advantage of the occasion to stage an abridged version of Annette's "Patrick" musical as the second half of the show with Shane O' Fearghail as Patrick and Sheila Canavan as the high kings daughter. Annette would have been so happy and proud that her music was at last being recognised and helping others to start a career in music. Incidentally that same week my own show "Sinatra, A Man And His Life" was staged for three nights in The Sugar Club.

Annette's music is the one big consolation I have in this lonely life I now lead. Some years ago she went into a small studio and recorded some of her compositions. Every day, as soon as I get up, I play that CD so that Annette's voice is still heard about the house. I have promised Annette that as long as I am alive and in the house, her voice will be heard in it every day.

Two years ago one of the things Joan Glennon said to me in the Plaza Hotel, and one of the things I laughed about with my friends, was that I would write a book about the past. Little did I know then that before a year was out Annette would be gone from my earthly life and that the book I would write with Annette's help would be this book, a memoir of our past.

I try to visit Annette's grave every day. I keep a candle lighting at all times as I want her to know that my love for her will burn as bright as the flame of the candle, and, until I am placed beside her in that grave on the hillside in Bohernabreena Cemetery, I will keep our love symbolised in that lighted candle, a light that will never go out as long as I am alive.

THE END